BOOKS BY NAT HENTOFF

MUSIC:

HEAR ME TALKING TO YA (with Nat Shapiro)

JAZZ (with Albert McCarthy)

JAZZ COUNTRY (for young readers)

THE JAZZ LIFE

THE JAZZ MAKERS (with Nat Shapiro)

JOURNEY INTO JAZZ (for very young readers)

NONFICTION:

THE NEW EQUALITY

OUR CHILDREN ARE DYING

PEACE AGITATOR: THE STORY OF A. J. MUSTE

A POLITICAL LIFE: THE EDUCATION OF JOHN V. LINDSAY

STATE SECRETS: POLICE SURVEILLANCE IN AMERICA

(with Paul Cowan and Nick Egleson)

NOVELS FOR ADULTS:

CALL THE KEEPER

ONWARDS!

NOVELS FOR YOUNG READERS:

I'M REALLY DRAGGED BUT NOTHING GETS ME DOWN

IN THE COUNTRY OF OURSELVES

THIS SCHOOL IS DRIVING ME CRAZY

jazz is

JAZZ

is

by nat hentoff

Limelight Editions New York 1984

photographs by bob parent

First Limelight Edition, March 1984
Text Copyright © 1976 by Nat Hentoff
Photographs copyright © 1976 by Bob Parent
All rights reserved under International and Pan-American Copyright Conventions. Published
in the United States by Proscenium Publishers Inc., New York, and simultaneously in Canada
by Fitzhenry & Whiteside Limited, Toronto.
Originally published by Random House, Inc., and The Ridge Press.

Sections of the chapters on Billie Holiday and
Miles Davis appeared, in different form, in the
New York Times Sunday Magazine, December 24, 1972 and April 14, 1974.
Copyright © 1972/1974 by The New York Times Company.

Parts of the chapter on Gerry Mulligan were first
printed, in different form, in *The New Yorker.*

Library of Congress Cataloging in Publication Data
Hentoff, Nat.
  Jazz is.
  Discography: p.
  Bibliography: p.
  Includes index.
  1. Jazz music.   I.   Title.
ML3561.J3H447   785.4'2   75-10329
ISBN 0–87910–003–6
Manufactured in the United States of America

For all the creators of this
spirit-music—especially, in memory of the
nonpareil nonpareil, Duke Ellington. And also for
Frankie Newton, Rex Stewart, Red Allen, Pee
Wee Russell, and Herbie Nichols.

introduction

As a boy, they seemed to me a different species. I could ask a ballplayer or a movie star for an autograph, but I was speechless when Johnny Hodges or Lester Young walked by. I was in awe of jazz musicians because of their power, because of the mystery of their sinuous but overwhelming power. Nothing else in my experience was so exhilarating, so utterly compelling. The laughter in the music, the intimacy, the range and bite of the life-tales each player told in textures and cadences entirely his own. The irony, the deep blues, and, as I grew older, the sensuousness.

Also, as I grew older, I was finally able to speak and get to know scores of these magical improvisers. And then scores more. I remained—and still am—in awe of the leaping imagination of the best of them. Off the stand they are, of course, like us, variously flawed. And yet to me they are still a different species. I have covered many beats through the years—civil liberties, education, classical and folk music, rock, the courts, films and theater, politics—and still, by and large, I most enjoy being with jazz musicians.

For one thing, they have little patience with euphemism, since they spend much of their working time being direct. Also, being accustomed to change as the only constant in their music, they tend to be more resilient and curious than most—and less likely to be conned by the manipulative conventional wisdom of institutions and institutional figures. And, as you might expect, most jazz people are lively, irreverent, sharp-witted. They see as well as hear a lot.

This book is a selective tribute and guide to the jazz life, the players, and the music. It is not a chronological or a comprehensive history, but rather a personal exploration through variegated seminal figures of the nature of the music (and how it keeps changing). And it is about the nature of those who make the music—temperaments as disparate as those of Louis Armstrong and Charlie Parker. It tells too of the political economy of jazz, its internationalization, the continuing surprises of its further frontiers.

I have been writing about this music for some thirty years, and since I am not a musicologist my approach has been to try to understand the intertwining of lives and sounds, of personal styles and musical styles, of societal dynamics and jazz dynamics. I still find it ceaselessly absorbing—the music, its players, and the society which thinks them marginal as they illuminate it so penetratingly and sometimes so mordantly.

Above all, however, this book is meant to bring pleasure—to bring you to the music of these players and composers, if you have not been there before, and perhaps suggest another dimension if you have been.

I am grateful to all the players in this book for the conversation, as well as musical time, they've given me through the years. They are a brilliant motley, each having lived—or still living—a life obsessed with this spirit-music, its mysteries and infinite seductiveness. And the magnetism works both ways, of course. Once you're inside the music you'll want to keep going deeper and deeper, because it is impossible to get enough of it.

—Nat Hentoff
New York City

jazz is:

A cold winter afternoon in Boston, and I, sixteen, am passing the Savoy Cafe in the black part of town. A slow blues curls out into the sunlight and pulls me indoors. **Count Basie,** hat on, with a half smile, is floating the beat with **Jo Jones's** brushes whispering behind him. Out on the floor, sitting on a chair which is leaning back against a table, **Coleman Hawkins** fills the room with big, deep, bursting sounds, conjugating the blues with the rhapsodic sweep and fervor he so loves in the opera singers whose recordings he plays by the hour at home.

     The blues goes on and on as the players turn it round and round and inside out and back again, showing more of its faces than I had ever thought existed. I stand, just inside the door, careful not to move and break the priceless sound. In a way I am still standing there.

Guitarist **Jim Hall,** a shy man whose whole life, practically, is jazz, saying to critic Whitney Balliett: "I've always felt that the music started out as black but that it's as much mine now as anyone else's. I haven't stolen the music from anybody—I just bring something different to it."

Max Roach, master modern drummer: "Black musicians play black music."

Pee Wee Russell, who played jazz with every inch of his thin, elongated body and thereby appeared to be made of rubber as he stretched and twisted during a solo, had a sound unlike that of any other clarinetist in jazz. He made the clarinet growl, rasp, squeak (most of the time deliberately), and then suddenly the horn would whisper, sensuously, delicately, promising even more swirling intimacies to come. And never, ever, was it possible to predict the shapes of what was to come.

One night, in the late 1940's, a student from the New England Conservatory of Music came into a jazz room in Boston where Pee Wee was playing, went up to the stand, and unrolled a series of music manuscript pages. They were covered, densely, with what looked like the notes of an extraordinarily complex, ambitious classical composition.

"I brought this for you," the young man said to Pee Wee Russell. "It's one of your solos from last night. I transcribed it."

Pee Wee, shaking his head, looked at the manuscript. "This can't be me," he said. "I can't play this."

The student assured Pee Wee that the transcribed solo, with its fiendishly brilliant structure and astonishingly sustained inventiveness, was indeed Russell's.

"Well," Pee Wee said, "even if it is, I wouldn't play it again the same way—even if I could, which I can't."

Billie Holiday, toward the end of her life, tired, playing a gig where the money was bad, the audience uncertain. Her voice hoarse and cracked, she starts to speak more than sing the verse to a song. But her beat is so pulsatingly supple, her phrasing so evocatively hornlike, that her speech is music, and the audience is caught in her time.

Duke Ellington, saying to me: "The other night I heard a cat on the radio, and he was talking about 'modern' jazz. So he played a record to illustrate his point, and there were devices in that music I heard cats using in the 1920's. These large words like 'modern' don't *mean* anything. Everybody who's had anything to say in this music—all the way back—has been an individualist. I mean musicians like Sidney Bechet, Louis Armstrong, Coleman Hawkins. Then what happens is that hundreds of other musicians begin to be shaped by that one man. They fall in behind him and you've got what people call a category. But I don't listen in terms like 'modern' jazz. I listen for those individualists. Like Charlie Parker was."

Rex Stewart, long with Duke Ellington, and then, for a time, an exile in white farm country in upstate

New York. A couple of memories of those Stewart years by a friend of Rex, Darwin Skinner: "One afternoon I was at a pickup jazz session up there, and all of a sudden I heard the most beautiful cornet. This man was walking up the aisle of the inn playing his heart out. I had never heard such playing before or since. It was, I discovered, Rex Stewart. He had bought a farm and was going to be in seclusion, but he couldn't stop playing. Shortly after, we were in a town there with a grill called the Crystal Lounge, where there were occasional sessions. On the street I found Rex looking into the Crystal Lounge with his nose almost pressed against the window. He turned and asked me almost as a favor to accompany him into the grill. He didn't want to walk in alone because he was black. You can imagine my pride walking into this white jazz scene with one of the greatest musicians of our time.

"At another place where Rex went on to play, I'd come often, and I could hear his horn grow more bitter with each passing night. The notes did not cry for help but shouted in anger at the way the world was treating Rex Stewart." But the world, of course, didn't know it was being addressed by Rex.

Sam Rivers, an authentic jazz original, as reedman, teacher, and composer, saying in the New York Jazz Museum's booklet, *Billie Holiday Remembered:* "In the fall of 1956, I was on the verge of a nervous breakdown. I decided to go to Miami. Billie Holiday was there, Cab Calloway, King Cole, Dinah Washington, B. B. King, Ray Charles, Chet Baker. . . . After work everyone would go to the Sir John Motel to jam until 8 or 9 in the morning. I played next to Billie. She'd just done a chorus and I took a solo. She told her piano player, Carl Drinkard, that she liked the way I played. Then I had an attack, broke out in cold sweat, felt faint. Billie noticed and told me to go outside; she'd watch my horn. She said she'd watched Pres' horn for him when he had to go out.

"When I came back she was singing 'Detour Ahead.' I listened to the anguish in her voice and the lyrics seemed to be about my own problems. I started to cry."

Jimmy Rowles, the Gerald Moore of jazz

accompanists, and a soloist so perennially fresh and lucid in conception—with flawless, floating time—that he has long been a musicians' favorite, talking of how he left the security of the West Coast studios in his mid-fifties: "A few months ago, I suddenly started thinking, 'Why did you take up the piano in the first place?' Because I wanted to play my own way. And out there, in Los Angeles, free-lancing in the studios and doing jingles and the like, I never got to.

"Now's the time, I thought, to try it. I'm ready to stay right with playing my own way. I don't want to be a millionaire. I just want to make a living playing the way I want to, and maybe making some people happy at the same time. The noise in the clubs doesn't bother me a bit. If I can find one person in the room who digs what I'm playing—and I can tell by looking at the way he or she is listening—that vibration is enough for me.

"As for where I'll go after this gig is over, well, it's like it always is in jazz, I suppose the phone will ring."

Martin Williams, writing in *The Jazz Tradition:*
"The high degree of individuality, together with
the mutual respect and cooperation required in a
jazz ensemble, carry with them philosophical
implications. . . . It is as if jazz were saying to us
that not only is far greater individuality possible to
man than he has so far allowed himself, but that
such individuality, far from being a threat to a
cooperative social structure, can actually enhance
society."

Jo Jones, "the man who plays like the wind," as
used to be said of him when he was with the Count
Basie band at its smoothly swinging zenith in the
1930's and '40's, is fond of lecturing younger jazz
musicians about the nature and responsibility of
their calling: "What is jazz? The closest I can get to
answering that is to say that jazz is playing what
you feel. All jazz musicians express themselves
through their instruments and they express the

types of persons they are, the experiences they've had during the day, during the night before, during their lives. There is no way they can subterfuge their feelings.

"It is like some guy will say with a great big smile, 'Man, I dig you the most,' and he'll start playing something that sounds entirely different. That's the same reaction an audience has sometimes. They may never have heard a man play before, and yet, when he brings his experiences onto the bandstand, he projects his feelings amongst the audience and he can either have them going out of the place smiling or in frowns. And that can prove disastrous after they get home because music, being the kind of medium it is, can affect you all your life."

Miles Davis, asked about standards in jazz, and saying: "I think all the musicians in jazz should get together on one certain day and get down on their knees to thank Duke."

the man who was an orchestra

Duke Ellington

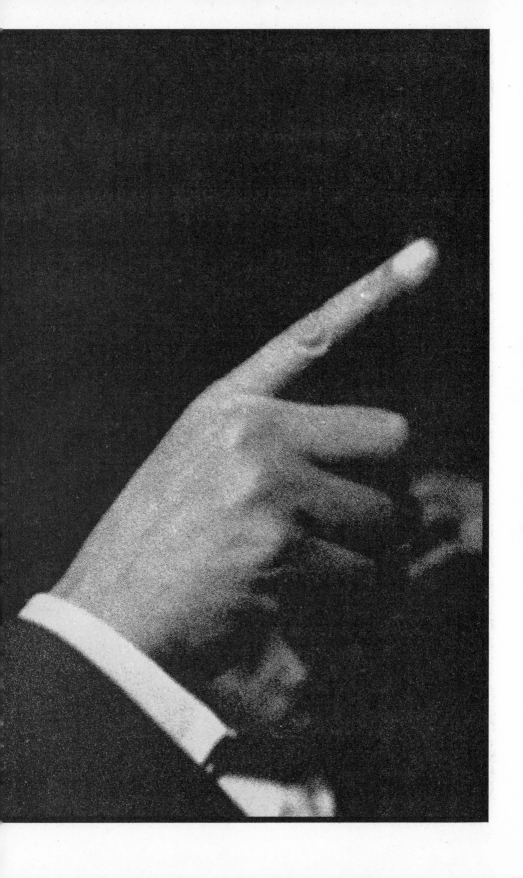

Count Basie

Whitney Balliett, jazz critic for *The New Yorker*, has called jazz "the sound of surprise." And it is that expectation of surprise, the sharing of the risk of unpredictability, which partly explains the compelling hold of jazz on listeners in just about every country in the world.

Most of us lead or are led by lives of patterned regularity. Diurnally, surprises are relatively few. And except for economic or physical uncertainties, we neither face nor court significant degrees of risk because a fundamental drive in the vast majority of us is toward the attainment of as much security as is possible.

In this sense, jazzmen, of all musicians, are our surrogates for the unpredictable, our paladins of constant change.

"It's like going out there naked every night," a bass player once said to me. "Any one of us can screw the whole thing up because he had a fight with his wife just before the gig or because he's just not with it that night for any number of reasons. I mean, we're out there *improvising*. The classical guys have their scores, whether they have them on stand or have memorized them. But we have to be creating, or trying to, anticipating each other, transmuting our feelings into the music, taking chances every goddamned second. That's why, when jazz musicians are really putting out, it's an exhausting experience. It can be exhilarating, too, but always there's that touch of fear, that feeling of being on a very high wire without a net below."

And jazz musicians who work with the more headlong innovators in the music face special hazards. There is the challenge, for instance, of staying in balance all the way in performances with Thelonious Monk as he plunges through, in, underneath, and around time. "I got lost one night," a

Monk sideman told me, "and I felt like I had just fallen into an elevator shaft."

There is another dimension of jazz surprise, the kind and quality that Duke Ellington exemplified. It is true that during many of his concerts and other appearances, Duke would schedule familiar numbers from his repertory for parts of the evening, sometimes long parts. He felt this an obligation to those who had come to see him, sometimes over long distances, and wanted to hear their favorites. Duke, who had come up in the business (and jazz is also a business) at a time when, to most of its audiences, the music was show business rather than art, considered it rude to present an audience with a program of entirely unfamiliar work.

But for Duke himself the continual and keenest pleasure in music was the continual surprising of himself. Always he was most interested in the new, the just completed work.

"The man," the late Billy Strayhorn said of Duke, for whom he became a musical alter ego, "is a constant revelation. He's continually renewing himself through his music. He's thoroughly attuned to what's going on *now*. He not only doesn't live in the past. He rejects it, at least so far as his own past accomplishments are concerned. He hates talking about the old bands and the old pieces. He has to play some of the Ellington standards because otherwise the audiences would be disappointed. But he'd much rather play the new things."

Duke never could stop composing. Even toward the end, in the hospital, his strength decimated by cancer, Ellington was still composing. And throughout his life, the corollary challenge and incomparable satisfaction for him was in the way he composed for the specific members of his orchestra.

"After a man has been in the band for a while," Ellington once told me, "I can hear what his capacities are, and I write to that. And I write to each man's sound. A man's sound is his total personality. I hear that sound as I prepare to write. I hear all their sounds, and that's how I am able to write. Before you can play anything or write anything, you have to hear it.

"Now," Ellington continued with enthusiasm, "the fun, the challenge is solving problems. Take *Boy Meets Horn*. There's one note with a cocked valve on the trumpet that has that sound I wanted—E natural. The big problem was to employ that note logically and musically within the overall structure of a composition. It was something to have fun with. It has nothing to do with conquering the world. You write it tonight and play it tomorrow, and that's it."

Not quite. There were many things Duke wanted to say, not just for tonight. *Black, Brown and Beige, Such Sweet Thunder, Harlem,* and hundreds, thousands more. Portraits of Willie "The Lion" Smith and Sidney Bechet and Bert Williams. *What Am I Here For?, Black Beauty, Rocks in My Bed, The Flaming Sword, Harlem Air Shaft.* A prodigious life's work lasting far beyond that life. But he did take care to point up the fun of it, the craft of it, for he was proud of his skills, and who had more reason to be?

"For a long time," Duke told me, "there was a lot of fun in writing for musicians who had weaknesses. You could astonish them with their strengths. Then it came to be that young musicians could play anything you set down. I remember, from before, when cats with trombones used to say, 'Man, this thing ain't got no keys on it, you know.' Now they don't say it; they just play it. So, the problems of writing for individual musicians with their particular advantages and their particular weaknesses are reduced. As a result, you try to make new problems for yourself another way. You try to think in terms of combinations, mixtures of timbres, sections of sections. It's gotten so adult and civilized and that sort of thing. The other way, the old way, was like a kid playing with blocks. The first time he sees a Q, he says, 'Now what'll we do with this?' He hasn't perhaps gotten beyond A, B, and C in his alphabet up to that point."

The old way, and all the continually searching new ways, had one constant foundation. As Billy Strayhorn said, "Ellington plays the piano, but his real instrument is his band. Each member of the band is to him a distinctive play of tone colors and a distinctive set of emotions; and he mixes them all into his own style. By writing specifically for each of his men, and thereby letting them play naturally and relaxed, Ellington is able to probe the intimate recesses of their minds and find things that not even the musicians knew were there."

And having written—late at night in hotel rooms; in the car, on scraps of paper, between dates; wherever he was when not fronting the band—Ellington was able to hear the results immediately. And that was his greatly enduring, continually self-regenerating satisfaction. Duke often told me that he considered the fate of most classical composers poignant. "They write and write and keep putting what they've done in a drawer and maybe, once in a great while, some orchestra will perform one of their works. The rest—they have to imagine, only imagine, what they've written sounds like. I could not exist that way, creating music only for myself, not communicating with anyone but myself. But having an orchestra always with me makes it unnecessary for me to wait." Duke did not have to travel constantly; he could have lived comfortably on the royalties from his abundance of compositions. But he greatly preferred the road so that he could hear his music, especially his new music, instantly. Or, as he put it, "I keep these expensive gentlemen with me to gratify that desire."

Duke professed to be unconcerned with prizes and awards for, after all, he received his essential psychic income from writing for those "expensive gentlemen." Yet, he was exacerbated—as many jazz musicians have been and continue to be—at the rather low estate to which jazz is relegated by the American "cultural establishment."

We were talking once about his never having been awarded a Pulitzer Prize for music. In 1965 an attempt had indeed been made to cite Ellington for a token special award "for the vitality and originality of his total productivity" (not the full-fledged Pulitzer itself). But the three-man music jury which had suggested so slight a break with the Pulitzer tradition was overruled, and two of them resigned in protest. At the time Duke said publicly, "Fate is being kind to me. Fate doesn't want me to be too famous too young."

To a friend he said: "I'm hardly surprised that my kind of music is still without, let us say, official honor at home. Most Americans still take it for granted that European-based music—classical music, if you will—is the only really respectable kind." [Most Americans of middle and later years think that way, but many of the young are of another persuasion. N.H.]

Duke recalled that "when Franklin Roosevelt died, practically no American music was played on the air in tribute to him. We, our band, were given a dispensation, however. We did one radio program, during the period of mourning, dedicated to him. But by and large, jazz was then and always has been like the kind of man you wouldn't want your daughter to associate with.

"The *word* 'jazz' has been part of the problem," Ellington continued. "The word never lost its association with those New Orleans bordellos. In the 1920's I used to try to convince Fletcher Henderson that we ought to call what we were doing 'Negro music.' But it's too late for that now. The music has become so integrated you can't tell one part from the other so far as color is concerned."

But in Ellington's music the basic color was always black. Although some white musicians were in the band from time to time, Ellington's compositions—whether based on Shakespeare or conceived as sound-photographs of the Far East—always were based on a black perspective. As Cecil Taylor, one of the many performer-composers whom Duke has deeply and lastingly influenced, said in the late 1950's: "He showed me how it was possible to incorporate all kinds of musical and other influences as part of my life as an American Negro. Everything I've lived I am in my music. And that's true of Duke, too."

An inescapable part of Ellington's life was his acute, abiding awareness of racism. Because he seldom spoke out on the issue—he preferred his public speech to be gracefully unsubstantive—Duke was wrongly thought by some through the years to be insensitive to what used to be called Jim Crow.

"People who think that of me," Duke told me years ago (when the term "Negro" had not been supplanted by "black"), "have not been listening to our music. For a long time, social protest and pride in the Negro have been the most significant themes in what we've done. In that music we have been talking for a long time about what it is to be a Negro in this country. And we've never let ourselves be put into a position of being treated with disrespect. From 1934 to 1936 we went touring deep into the South, without the benefit of Federal judges, and we commanded respect. We didn't travel by bus. Instead, we had two Pullman cars and a 70-foot baggage car. We parked them in each station, and lived in them. We had our own water, food, electricity, and sanitary facilities. The natives would come by and say, 'What's that?' 'Well,' we'd say, 'that's the way the President travels.'

"We made our point," Duke continued. "What else could we have done at that time? In the years since, we've done more benefits for civil-rights groups than anybody, but still the best way for me to be effective is through music."

(Years later, an experience of Cecil Taylor sharply reminded me of what Ellington had said. In the late 1960's Taylor was teaching and developing a student orchestra at Antioch College. During a series of demonstrations at Antioch by black students and some white allies—aimed, among other things, at getting more black low-income students into the college—the campus was shut down. Taylor continued his rehearsals at a place outside the campus and was excoriated by some of the black leaders of the rebellion for not shutting down his classes.

("When are you going to start doing something for your people?" one of them roared at Taylor.

("I've been doing that in my music all my life," Taylor answered accurately.)

Trumpeter Clark Terry has described the quintessential jazz nature of Duke Ellington: "He wants life and music to be always in a state of becoming. He doesn't even like to write definitive endings to a piece. He'd often ask us to come up with ideas for closings, but when he'd settled on one of them, he'd keep fooling with it. He always likes to make the end of a song sound as if it's still going somewhere."

Accordingly, an Ellington recording session was always a kaleidoscope of the unexpected, a seemingly perpetual "state of becoming." As Duke himself once said of those sessions, "When we're all working together a guy may have an idea and he plays it on his horn. Another guy may add to it and make something out of it. Someone may play a riff and ask, 'How do you like this?' The trumpets may try something together and say, 'Listen to this.' There may be a difference of opinion on what kind of mute to use. Someone may advocate extending a note or cutting it off. The sax section may want to put an additional smear on it."

The search for the exact kind of mute, it should be noted, was indicative of Ellington's conception of jazz writing and playing. Starting in the 1920's, as British musicologist Wilfrid Mellers has pointed out, Ellington became preoccupied "with the sonorous variety possible through the use of different types of mute—as an extension of jazz's traditional concern with melodic inflections as a kind of human speech; each man must reveal more of himself, through his own accent or dialect, and in so doing will make the richer contribution to the whole."

Through the decades, creating for the distinctively individual instrumental voices in the band and, of course, for the equally distinctive collective personality of the band, Ellington devised his own musical microcosm which had its own life, its own extraordinarily cohesive continuum. Like Bach,

Ellington worked in a multitude of forms—stretching them, transmuting them, interrelating them all in a spectrum of expression with its own logic of evolution, expansion, continual generation. It was far and away the single most important body of work in the history of jazz.

There is no way to label what Ellington created, except as his. And because his musicians were so integral a part of how he wanted to express himself, Duke was intensely loyal to them. A good many years ago he was visibly furious (an extreme rarity) at a young man who was then head of *Down Beat*'s Chicago office. In Duke's band at the time was a heroin addict, and that night he had nodded off during the entire first set.

"It looks awful, Duke," the young critic said, "that guy sitting there, zonked out in public. Why don't you get rid of him?"

"Do you realize," Duke snapped, "that that man fought for you in the South Pacific, where he contracted a rare form of malaria which puts him in this condition from time to time?"

The blood of the musician in question would have instantly stunned any mosquito to death, but Duke was not about to have a citizen of his own principality criticized by an outsider.

Duke found it nearly impossible to fire one of his musicians. "He can't bring himself to do that," Billy Strayhorn told me. "He'll wait until it becomes obvious to the man himself that he'd be happier somewhere else. And sooner or later the man leaves."

A veteran Ellington sideman said: "He was no disciplinarian, which is not to say that he hung out with us. He'd kid around with us, but if you got too close to him, he'd make a joke or put you on, and edge away. And once in a while he would show displeasure at one of us. But obliquely. Like if you came in after having too much to drink, he'd call for the most difficult piece in the book featuring *you*."

There was another Ellington way of manifesting annoyance, which I used to see and hear at Ellington dances from the time I was a boy. He would sometimes bang hard on the piano either to underline the fact that a wrong note had just been played by someone or, if a musician had been late returning after intermission, to advise him that his presence was required instantly.

Duke did fire one man—Charles Mingus, who had just joined the band for an engagement at the Apollo Theater in Harlem. Backstage, trombonist Juan Tizol, an elder Ellington sideman, had criticized the way Mingus was playing a piece Tizol had written. The subsequent intemperate dialogue had at first resulted in Mingus chasing Tizol away, but then, as the curtain rose to the sound of *Take the A Train*, Tizol rushed out onstage, lunging at Mingus with a bolo knife.

Ellington's subsequent dismissal of Mingus, reported in the latter's book, *Beneath the Underdog/His World as Composed by Mingus*, is a superbly accurate account of how, when he could no longer avoid it, the determinedly urbane Ellington confronted unpleasantness: "'Now, Charles,' he says, looking amused, putting Cartier links into the cuffs of his beautiful handmade shirt, 'you could have forewarned me—you left me out of the act entirely! At least you could have let me cue in a few chords as you ran through that Nijinsky routine. I congratulate you on your performance, but why didn't you and Juan inform me about the adagio you planned so that we could score it? I must say I never saw a large man so agile—I never saw *anybody* make such tremendous leaps! The gambado over the piano carrying your bass was colossal. When you exited after that I thought, "That man's really afraid of Juan's knife and at the speed he's going he's probably home in bed by now." But no, back you came through the same door with your bass still intact. For a moment I was hopeful you'd decided to sit down and play but instead you slashed Juan's chair in two with a fire axe!

"'Really, Charles, that's destructive. Everybody knows Juan has a knife but nobody ever took it seriously—he likes to pull it out and show it to people, you understand. So I'm afraid, Charles—I've never fired anybody—you'll have to quit my band. I don't need any new problems. Juan's an old problem, I can cope with that, but you seem to have a whole bag of new tricks. I must ask you to be kind enough to give me your notice, Mingus.'"

"I was amazed," a musician who was in the band at the time told me, "that Duke actually did fire Mingus. I thought he'd wait at least until Mingus had split Juan Tizol's head open."

Ellington's chronic tendency to shy from unpleasantness may have been due in part to his having been so sedulously sheltered from unpleasantness as he was growing up. As he wrote of his parents in *Music Is My Mistress* (speaking of himself in the third person): "They loved their little boy very much. They raised him, nurtured him, coddled him, and spoiled him. They raised him in the palm of the hand and gave him everything they thought he wanted. Finally, when he was about seven or eight, they let his feet touch the ground."

In any case, Duke did consider life as a gift to be

savored as fully as possible and saw no sense in corroding it with any more worry than was absolutely necessary. He was fond of saying, "Do you know the difference between worry and concern? Worry is destructive, but concern is a thinking mind solving a problem."

One of the reasons he delighted in traveling—the lot of the jazzman—was that when you're moving, worries can't collect around you. "When I'm riding in the car with Harry," Duke would say, referring to baritone saxophonist Harry Carney, who had been with him since 1926 and who died only a few months after him, "there's this marvelous freedom from telephone calls and all kinds of business. Harry and I don't talk much, so I can just dream and write."

There were other pleasures in the continuous traveling required to keep the band working all year long. "After all," Duke told me, "I do what other people do when they go on vacation. In addition, I have friends everywhere. Also, by being in so many different places and getting a chance to talk to so many different people, I know what's going on—long before any commentator in Washington or wherever.

"And the traveling," he continued, in terms I've heard other jazz musicians use, "is a stimulus for the music. What I'm involved in is a continuing autobiography, a continuing record of the people I meet, the places I see and then see change. Furthermore, what is music if it isn't communication? I like to *know* firsthand what the response is to what I write. And it's by playing all these one-nighters that I can hear reactions from all kinds of audiences. You get real contact when you play a phrase and somebody sighs. Moreover, there's that other kind of contact that gives me constant pleasure. Harry and I are driving into a new state and one of us will say, 'I wonder if so-and-so and his wife will drive that hundred miles to see us *this* time.' You get to the date, look up, and they're there. It's a great experience, having Iowa farmers drive two hundred miles to hear you in January, or going back to England and having people in every town show you programs from 1933, or whenever you last played there. That sort of thing you can't buy. That sort of thing keeps you young."

While life on the road has traditionally enabled many jazz players to greatly expand their social lives, partying after work, Duke was seldom drawn to that dividend of the itinerant musician's opportunities. "Duke would much rather sit up and write after work than go to a party," Billy Strayhorn often said. "I'm used to his calling me at 8 or 9 in the morning to talk over a musical problem that's just developed or to tell me about a piece he's been up all night writing."

On occasion, particularly in New York, where he was more or less based, Duke did go out to hear particular musicians. He would never criticize any of them. "I'm not good at appraisals," Duke would say. But if he liked someone, he would try to help, in his oblique way. Pianist Marian McPartland, many years ago, had a long run at the Hickory House in New York where Duke spent much of his off-time in the city. She came off the stand one night to find Ellington there and he said, with a large smile, "You play so many notes." It took several months, Marian McPartland recalls, for that to sink in. "I was green as grass, but I suddenly realized he was telling me to edit myself. And of course he was right."

Music was his mistress, Duke said, and he seldom talked for long about anything else. There was certainly never any expectation by those who knew him that Ellington would retire.

"What would I do sitting in one place?" he would ask rhetorically. "How would I see all my friends? And how would I get to hear the new things I write? I'm in contact every night with people—live people—listening to my music. What *reasons* would I have for retiring from the road?"

And Duke never did retire. He kept moving, kept writing, kept savoring being alive, kept enjoying—in his elegantly mocking way—the seemingly endless chances to flick an edge of fun into all manner of circumstances. As when, toward the end of Lyndon Johnson's presidency, there was a plane ride so that Lady Bird could say good-by to America. The plane was full of security personnel; and Duke at one point leaned over to a political figure he knew and whispered, quite audibly, "Would you like some grass?"

And no one in jazz has ever been so graceful a master of the put-on as Duke. The last time I saw him I was standing, listening to the band. For some reason Duke was not on stand. I felt my shoulder being tapped and then I heard the voice.

"You don't know who I am," Edward Kennedy Ellington said, "but I know who you are."

Millions throughout the world knew who Duke was. He touched so many lives in ways that he could never have known about. At his funeral on May 27, 1974, at the Cathedral of St. John the Divine in New York, there were thousands of mourners, inside and outside the church. One of them, a black man, no celebrity, just a man who lives in Harlem, said: "I'm just here to bear witness. A man passed through, and he was a giant."

A giant who throve on the sounds—the sounds beyond category—that he created. Only death could retire him. Some years ago, as the band was setting up for a concert,

38

I was talking to one of Duke's sidemen about how Duke was bearing up under the rigors of the road now that he was in his seventies. "Oh," the musician said, "he doesn't consider them 'rigors.' Quite the opposite. He knows that if he were to stop traveling with the band he'd be just like Dorian Gray. He'd age overnight. No, he'll be out there as long as he can move. He's found the way to stay young. Watch him some night in the wings. Those bags under his eyes are huge, and he looks beat and kind of lonely. But then we begin to play, he strides out on the stand, the audience turn their faces to him, and the cat is a new man."

A sense of the perdurable impact of Duke Ellington was given by Stanley Dance, the British-born jazz critic and longtime friend of Duke, in his eulogy at Ellington's funeral: "Of all the cities he conquered—more than Napoleon, and by much better methods—I remember particularly Buenos Aires when he went there the first time. He had played his final concert and sat in the car outside the theater before going to the airport. People clutched at him through the opened windows, people who were crying, who thrust gifts on him, gifts on which they hadn't even written their names. It was one of the few times I saw him moved to tears."

jazz is:

John Hammond, remembering: "I first heard
Billie in early 1933. She was seventeen, and she'd
been scarred by life already. . . . She was the first
girl singer I'd come across who actually sang like
an improvising jazz genius—an extension, almost,
of Louis Armstrong. The way she sang around a
melody, her uncanny harmonic sense and her sense
of lyric content were almost unbelievable in a girl
of seventeen. And her time was something else."

Roy Eldridge: "Billie must have come from
another world because nobody had the effect on
people she had. She could really get to people. I've
seen her make them cry and make them happy."

Bobby Tucker (Billie Holiday's accompanist for

some years): "With most singers you have to guide
them and carry them along—they're either laying
back or else running away from you. But not Billie
Holiday. Man, it was a thrill to play for her. She
had the greatest conception of a beat I ever heard.
It just didn't matter what kind of song she was
singing. She could sing the fastest tune in the
world or else something that was like a dirge, but
you could take a metronome and she'd be right
there. Hell, with Lady you could relax while you
were playing for her. You could damn near forget
the tune."

Miles Davis: "I'd rather hear her with Bobby
Tucker. . . . She doesn't need any horns. She
sounds like one, anyway."

lady day

Billie Holiday

Lester Young

Part of the power of jazz is its spontaneity, its directness— again, its sound of surprise.

Dizzy Gillespie's big band, at Birdland in New York. Coming down the stairs I heard a crackling, stunning trumpet cadenza, brilliant in content as well as in its reckless virtuosity. And yet it wasn't Dizzy. I looked at the stand and there was a teenager from Philadelphia, Lee Morgan, for whom Dizzy had just opened the door to the Big Apple.

Another night at a rather sleazy but congenial Greenwich Village bar, Cafe Bohemia. Like Birdland, it was a room where musicians were always in attendance at the bar, sometimes even at the tables. And like Birdland it was a place where unknown musicians, if courage seized them, tried to initiate their reputations.

Donald Byrd, just come to the Big Apple from Detroit, first established himself at the Bohemia, playing trumpet with such quicksilver grace that, as a waitress put it one night, "My God, he's the first jazz hummingbird I've heard."

And this night, a large young man from Florida, his alto saxophone looking like a toy against his girth, ascended the stand to sit in. He was Julian "Cannonball" Adderley. To test this uncommonly confident, even brash, young man, the leader, Oscar Pettiford, set off a tempo on *I'll Remember April* that might have intimidated even Art Tatum. Adderly more than survived that set and the very next day he got a call for his first record date—on Savoy. Not as a sideman, but as a leader.

Another night—and each jazz listener anywhere in the world has experienced comparable nights of sudden revelation—Sonny Stitt was playing at a club called Basin Street West in New York. The lore had it that Sonny was Charlie Parker's successor, that Bird had actually told him so. But Sonny, though technically fluent and certainly a steady swinger, had shown little of Bird's careening imagination or his ability to hurl an audience into new dimensions of feeling time and musical space.

This night Sonny Stitt was moving efficiently through a set when the rhythm section stopped—and Sonny executed a long break, lightning flashes of searing, ineluctably connected, thrusting notes that seemed to have a palpable force. The effect on the room was as if those sounds had cast a spell. All conversation stopped. Hands about to light a cigarette or reaching for a drink froze.

In jazz you never know what's coming.

In December, 1957, Whitney Balliett and I were asked by CBS television producer Robert Herridge to assemble musicians for what Herridge wanted to be the most authentic hour of jazz yet seen and heard on television. One decision we came to early was that there would be a minimum of script. As John Coltrane was to tell me years later, "I really wish there were no liner notes on my albums. If the music doesn't say it, how can words say it *for* the music?"

We also agreed that there would be no sets. Again, it was the music—and those who made it—that told it all, visually as well as aurally. And so the studio was our set, including the cameramen. Jazz doesn't pretend. So why should we? If a cameraman were caught in another cameraman's shot, so what? It was, after all, a television show.

Furthermore, why shouldn't the musicians be as comfortable as they'd be at an after-hours jam session? And so we told them to wear what was most comfortable and natural for them. Some, like Coleman Hawkins, wore their hats as they would at a recording session or when playing after hours. (Later I was severely criticized for this by a superior jazz alto saxophonist and arranger who had, however, internalized the bourgeois concept of how jazz players *should* look if the music were ever to be "respectable." This black alto player was furious at the fact that the jazz musicians on this program, *The Sound of Jazz*, had entered people's homes throughout the country with their hats on! I never was able to persuade him that dignity is not a matter of dress but of what you do and how well you do it.)

On the program was Billie Holiday—from whom no one ever quite knew what to expect. When I first told her that we were going natural, she was bristlingly angry. "I just spent five hundred goddam dollars on a gown!" she complained. But after the first rundown on camera—so the cameramen could get some sense of what was going to be demanded of them— Billie began to enjoy the unpressured ambience of the proceedings.

As the program itself started, the musicians were seen smoking and talking with each other (when they themselves weren't playing) and Billie, wearing slacks, her hair in a ponytail, made her entrance walking merrily through the ranks of the Count Basie band, kidding some of her longtime colleagues as she ambled along.

On this Sunday afternoon, less than two years before Billie's death, she was about to sing *Fine and Mellow*. Perched on a high stool she faced a semicircle of musicians who were all standing—except one, Lester Young. Prez (as Billie had nicknamed him long before) was sick. He had been so weak during the run-throughs that most of his solos during a previous segment with Basie's band had been split between Ben Webster and Coleman Hawkins. Now Prez was slumped in a chair, his eyes averted from Billie, whom he had not spoken to for some time. Once they had been very close, and I didn't know what discord had kept them estranged for so long, but throughout the rehearsals they had ignored each other.

Lady Day began to sing; and in the darkened control room the producer, the director, and the technical staff leaned forward, some of them, as the performance got underway, mumbling expletives of wonder. The song, which Billie had written, was one of the few blues in her repertory, and this time she was using it to speak not so much of trouble but rather of the bittersweet triumph of having survived—with some kicks along the way. Despite the myth that, toward the end, Lady invariably sounded like a cracked husk of what she had been years before, when she would not sing without a gardenia in her hair, that afternoon she was in full control of the tart, penetrating, sinuously swinging instrument which was her voice.

It was time for Prez's solo. Somehow he managed to stand up, and then he blew the sparest, purest blues chorus I have ever heard. Billie, smiling, nodding to the beat, looked into Prez's eyes and he into hers. She was looking back, with the gentlest of regrets, at their past. Prez was remembering, too. Whatever had blighted their relationship was forgotten in the communion of the music. Sitting in the control room I felt tears, and saw tears on the faces of most of the others there. The rest of the program was all right, but this had been its climax—the empirical soul of jazz.

Later, a woman wrote in to the television network to say how startling it had been to see on television "*real* people, doing something that *really* matters to them."

For Billie Holiday, certainly, music mattered overwhelmingly. As jazz singer Carmen McRae, a friend of Billie's, once said to me about Lady Day: "Singing is the only place she can express herself the way she'd like to be all the time. The only time she's at ease and at rest with herself is when she sings. I mean when she *can* sing, not when she's under the influence of liquor or whatever she's on."

There is a certain hyperbole to what Carmen said. I remember times with Billie in a friend's house, talking on the street, in a dressing room, when she was at reasonable ease, usually sardonic but not malicious, and hilariously accurate in her imitations of bookers and managers and record producers and other panjandrums of the industry. But it was true, I think, that Billie felt best about herself, surest about herself, when she was singing. Or, as Carmen McRae put it, when she was able to sing.

And when she was able to sing she was in charge, whether it was a big band (in her relatively early years) or a small combo or trio. Trumpeter Buck Clayton has recalled: "When she joined Count Basie, we had to rehearse because of the big band, mostly for the horns. Oh, we had places for her to come in, but that was all. She would follow Lester Young or me. All she needed to know was when to come in and when to quit. Aside from that she'd sing the way she wanted to. Nobody could ever tell her *how* to sing. She sang the way she felt."

Billie survives, in sound and in memory, through her music. And yet for the public at large (many of whom know her only in distorted legend, such as in the Diana Ross movie *Lady Sings the Blues*), Billie is most remembered as a victim—of herself, of society. The rhythms she moved to were a junkie's beat, according to this legend. The real, more complex rhythms of her life and her music have become blurred.

So it has often been in jazz history. Legends float, bearing little relation to the specific gravity of the fabled figure being revered or voyeured. Many of those, for instance, who idealized Charlie Parker after his death knew little of him or his music, but were enchanted by their notion of this wild rebel whose insatiable independence caused "society" to "kill" him. Bird's life and music were more earthily tangled than that, just as Billie Holiday's art was much more than the extension of a ghostly victim.

Not that Billie was not a victim and was not hooked on drugs for much of the last eighteen years of her life. And she did come up hard, although she was all too vulnerable inside until the day she died. Her first hurt was her abandonment by her guitarist-father, Clarence Holiday, who always considered Billie an accident. ("She was just something I stole when I was fifteen," he said years later to another musician.)

Eleanora Fagan (her mother's name) or Holiday changed her name to Billie when she was young because Eleanora was "too damn long for anyone to say." She started scrubbing white folks' steps in Baltimore when she was six. She also ran errands for the madam and the other professionals in a whorehouse in return for being allowed to listen to Bessie Smith and Louis Armstrong records on the house Victrola; was almost raped at ten and put away in a Catholic institution as punishment, presumably for "enticement"; and left school at thirteen, having gone only as far as fifth grade.

"Up South" in New York (as Malcolm X characterized being black in the North), Billie worked briefly as a maid, a role she despised both then and in her one Hollywood picture, *New Orleans*, with Louis Armstrong. By the age of fifteen Billie was turning tricks in a brothel on 141st Street. ("I had someone doing *my* laundry," she notes in her book, *Lady Sings the Blues*, written with William Dufty). She was soon in jail again for having refused to accept a too-rugged customer who happened to be somewhat of a power in Harlem.

Because of that experience, and for reasons of pride,

Billie stopped turning tricks and began to sing in Harlem clubs. Her reputation grew rather swiftly, in part because of the proselytizing work of John Hammond, the Magellan of jazz (his finds having ranged over forty years from Count Basie and Charlie Christian to Bob Dylan).

"It was around 1933," Hammond told me, "and in a club uptown there was this chubby girl going around the tables, singing. I couldn't believe my ears. No chick I'd heard sounded like this—like an instrument, like Louis's trumpet. And the way she improvised. When those girls were working they had to sing a route which ran to twenty or thirty tables. That required an extraordinary amount of musical resourcefulness, and if you didn't have it that was clear right away. She had it."

Hammond also remembers that, although the other girls working the tables were expected to collect their tips by lifting their dresses and using their labia to pick up the dollar bills, Billie would not. It was at that point, by the way, that she first started to be called Lady, at first derisively by her less punctilious associates. Lester Young later expanded the sobriquet to Lady Day, taking the addition from her last name.

In 1933 John Hammond persuaded Benny Goodman to use the fifteen-year-old Harlem singer on a record date, Billie's first. Many more recordings followed, including a notable series of small band sessions under Teddy Wilson's direction. The recordings helped establish Billie, though not financially. "I made over two hundred sides between 1933 and 1944," she wrote in *Lady Sings the Blues*, "but I don't get a cent of royalties on any of them. They paid me twenty-five, fifty, or a top of seventy-five bucks a side, and I was glad to get it. . . . But royalties were still unheard of."

Although Billie was working New York clubs fairly

regularly, the monetary returns were slight from those sources, too. Consequently, she went on the road with Count Basie and then with Artie Shaw. Billie, traveling light, failed to make her fortune stringing one-nighters together, but she added to her store of experiences concerning the depth and diversity of Jim Crow in the American grain. Billie was angered and disgusted by bigotry, but her response was considerably more resilient and defiant than is apparent in the soap-opera movie which purports to be about her life.

There was the time the Basie band arrived in a small Southern town which didn't even have a "colored" hotel. Quartered at the home of the local black minister, the Basie band and Billie had just finished an idiomatic but nearly indigestible dinner. One of their number, a very light-skinned member of the orchestra, had been missing from the table. On the street they saw him jauntily emerge from the best white restaurant in town. He pretended not to recognize his co-workers; and Billie, placing herself in front of him, shouted for all the town to hear: "All right for you, Peola!" (Peola, elder readers may recall, was the young Negro woman who tried to pass for white in the then-popular movie, *Imitation of Life.*)

Back in New York Billie became a star, as she somewhat wryly put it, after two years at Barney Josephson's Cafe Society. When she left, as she also remembered, she was still making the $75 a week at which she started. But gradually Billie's price rose, and she could have been a moderately affluent woman if she had not become involved in a series of ruinous affairs with exploitative men, and if she had not acquired a most expensive drug habit.

I have neither the qualifications nor the inclination to try to explain the specific dynamics of Billie's penchant for self-destruction; but it is germane to cite a point made by Bobby Tucker. "There's one thing about Lady Day you won't believe," he said. "She had the most *terrible* inferiority complex." Billie put it another way. Speaking of her childhood—the attempted rape; the times she had been locked up while she was still in her teens; the lack, to put it mildly, of a secure sense of family—she emphasized that those experiences had left her feeling "like a damn cripple." And she always insisted on telling any man with whom she had a relationship of "the things that happened to me when I was a kid."

In any case, until the end Billie had a hard time believing she was a star, even a falling star. She would be genuinely, almost ingenuously, touched when someone told her how much her singing meant to him. I do not mean she ever lost, for any length of time, her stubborn pride. Quite the contrary. Billie would hoot at such myths about her, as in the movie of *Lady Sings the Blues,* that without the support of one good strong man, she would have had an even untimelier end. Of all the men she knew she said, "I was as strong, if not stronger, than any of them. And when it's that way you can't blame anybody but yourself."

Not always, but often, Billie retained her sardonic wit in the worst of times. And she also kept her sense of rage when she felt she was being victimized by forces for which she could not and would not take the blame. There was the persistent harassment of Billie, for example, by those police, Federal and local, who specialize in enforcing the narcotics laws. When she once went to a private sanitorium to kick the habit, and succeeded for a time, a narcotics agent appeared there on the day she left, relentlessly keeping track of her. Some of her arrests for drug possession were legitimate; others were not; and always she had the sense of being tailed. There's more than one kind of monkey that can be on your back.

What most galled and depressed Billie was her inability to work in New York clubs for twelve years after she had served a ten-month term for drug possession at the Federal Women's Reformatory at Alderson, West Virginia. At that time anyone with a police record was refused permission to work in any New York room where liquor is sold. Billie was in show business, although she was also an artist to those of us who believe that jazz is America's classical music. And she knew, as Lenny Bruce later knew, that an entertainer exiled from New York suffers extensive career damage. As she did.

The hounds of the narcotics squads, imbued with faith in irredeemable sin, pursued Billie quite literally to her deathbed. A friend of Billie's, and of mine, Maely Dufty, who was once Charlie Parker's manager, has described Billie's last days in the notes for an ESP album of Billie Holiday radio performances.

In June, 1959, her liver badly damaged, Billie was taken in a coma to Metropolitan Hospital, where she was placed in an oxygen tent. After twelve days she regained consciousness but "still remained on the critical list, having to be fed intravenously while receiving blood transfusions.

"One morning, nine hours after I had left her bedside the night before," Maely Dufty wrote, "I found her in a deep rage. . . . 'You watch, baby, they are going to arrest me in this damn bed.' And so they did. The night nurse claimed she had found a deck of heroin in Billie's handbag, which was hanging from a nail on the wall—six feet away from the bottom of her bed. It was virtually impossible for Billie—with hundreds of pounds of equipment strapped to her legs and arms for transfusions—to have moved one inch toward that wall. One hour later the police arrived and arrested Billie

Holiday in her hospital bed. Charge: use of narcotics."

Even assuming the police charge to have been accurate, what followed underlines Billie's long-held contention that to the authorities being a drug-user is to find oneself on "a one-way street."

"To make the arrest of a woman in a hospital bed seem more real," Maely Dufty continued, "the police confiscated her comic books, radio, magazines, a box of Whitman chocolates, and Italian ice cream, and then stationed two cops at the doorless tiny gray hospital room. When I screamed at the authorities that they could not arrest a woman on the critical list, I was told that problem had already been solved: Billy Holiday had been removed from the critical list."

The issue was soon academic. Billie died in that hospital bed. She was forty-four.

If that were all of Billie, or most of Billie—the victim of herself and of the authorities—the substance of the Holiday legend might indeed be legitimately restricted, though without present distortions, to the tale of the Black Lady of the Gardenias. A latter-day Camille of the jazz grottoes who lit her candle at both ends. But that way of fashioning legend leaves out the essence of Lady Day—her music.

This was a woman who was as deeply pervasive an influence on jazz singing as Louis Armstrong and Charlie Parker were on jazz instrumental playing. Though herself influenced by Armstrong and Bessie Smith ("Honey, I wanted her feeling and Louis's style"), Billie, by the time she was in her twenties, had created a way of singing that was unmistakably her own. Or, as Ralph Cooper, then the compere at Harlem's Apollo Theater, said years ago about Billie: "It ain't the blues. I don't know what it is, but you got to hear her."

Billie Holiday, for one thing, excelled all jazz singers who had preceded her in her ability to make the lyrics of a song (and some of the songs she was given to record were most ordinary) take on nuances of meaning and feeling that lifted whatever she sang to significance, to many levels of significance. And as John Hammond instantly recognized when she was seventeen, Billie did sing like a horn. ("I try to improvise like Prez, like Louis, or someone else I admire. I hate straight singing. I have to change a tune to my own way of doing it. That's all I know.") No singer in jazz, before or since, has phrased with such supple inventiveness, as well as with such graceful, illuminating wit. Although nonpareil as a speleologist of the poignancy of ballads, Billie could also be the blithest of mocking spirits. And there was also her timing— her risk-taking playing with the beat, as only the most assured jazz instrumentalists are able to bend time to their feelings.

All these qualities were fused into a storyteller who could make waitresses stand still, cash registers remain unrung, and bring musicians backing her to applaud—as happened at a Carnegie Hall concert shortly after she was released from the Federal Women's Reformatory.

This bardic quality was hers to the end. There were stumbling off-nights, but the later Lady Day could be more compellingly expressive than the younger lady of the gardenias. In his book, *The Reluctant Art*, Benny Green, a British musician turned essayist, noted of Billie's singing in the 1950's: "The trappings were stripped away, but where the process would normally leave only the husk of a fine reputation, it only exposed to view, once and for all, the true core of her art, her handling of a lyric. If the last recordings are approached with this fact in mind, they are seen to be, not the insufferable croaking of a woman already half-dead, but recitatives whose dramatic intensity becomes unbearable, statements as frank and tragic as anything throughout the whole range of popular art."

So it was that less than two years before her death Billie sang *Fine and Mellow* on *The Sound of Jazz* with such tender yet acrid power that we cried in the control room and Lester Young was lifted to his feet to, briefly, rejoin Lady Day's life and art. That scene is not in the movie *Lady Sings the Blues*. That scene is real, as Billie's music can still be so real an experience to those who go to the only remaining source, Lady Day's recordings, to find out who Billie Holiday was.

Of course, for many reasons I wish Billie—and not only her voice—were still present. I'd give a lot to hear her response to socialite Maureen McCluskey who, as reported in the *New York Times* by Charlotte Curtis, said at a benefit supper party after the premiere of *Lady Sings the Blues:* "Doesn't everbody look marvelous? Of course, if I could come back again after I die, I'd come back black."

I would expect that Lady's reaction to that costless fantasy probably could not be printed in the *New York Times*.

jazz is:

Dizzy Gillespie, Newport Jazz Festival, 1970, at a
celebration of Louis Armstrong's seventieth
birthday: "If it hadn't been for him, there
wouldn't have been none of us. I want to thank
Mr. Louis Armstrong for my livelihood."

Miles Davis: "Louis has been through all kinds of
styles. You know you can't play anything on a horn
that Louis hasn't played."

Roy Eldridge, on first hearing Louis Armstrong,
the Lafayette Theater, New York: "He started out
like a new book, building and building, chorus
after chorus, and finally reaching a full climax,
ending on his high F. It was a real climax—right,
clean, clear. The rhythm was rocking, and he had
that sound going along with it. Everybody was
standing up, including me."

Dicky Wells, on first hearing Louis Armstrong, in the mid-1920's, with Fletcher Henderson's band, New York: "You just wondered where a guy like that had come from."

Pops Foster, on being on the road with Louis Armstrong during the 1930's: "It was tough traveling through the South in those days. We had two white guys with us—the bus driver and Joe Glaser [Louis's manager]. If you had a colored bus driver back then, they'd lock you up in every little country town for 'speeding.' It was very rough finding a place to sleep in the South. You couldn't get into the hotel for whites, and the colored didn't have any hotels. You rented places in private homes, boardinghouses, and whorehouses. The food was awful and we tried to find places where we could cook. We carried a bunch of pots and pans around with us."

the onliest louis

Louis Armstrong

Dizzy Gillespie

When Louis Armstrong, summoned by King Oliver, came up to Chicago in the summer of 1922, Buster Bailey reports that "Louis upset Chicago. All the musicians came to hear Louis. What made Louis upset Chicago so? His execution, for one thing, and his ideas, his drive. Well, they didn't call it drive, they called it 'attack' at the time. Yes, that's what it was, man. They got crazy for his feeling."

His feeling. Even toward the end of his life, when many of the same tunes would be played night after night, month after month, Louis could still, as trombonist Trummy Young remembers, make a sideman cry.

His feeling. Billie Holiday, a young girl in Baltimore, listening to Louis' recordings: "He didn't say any words, but somehow it just moved me so. It sounded so sad and sweet, all at the same time. It sounded like he was making love to me. That's how I wanted to sing."

There has been no jazz musician so widely, deeply, durably influential as Louis. And no trumpet player who could do all he could do on the horn. Once, Louis told journalist Gilbert Millstein, "I'm playin' a date in Florida, livin' in the colored section and I'm playin' my horn for *myself* one afternoon. A knock come on the door and there's an old, gray-haired flute player from the Philadelphia Orchestra, down there for his health. Walking through that neighborhood, he heard this horn, playing *Cavalleria Rusticana*, which he said he never heard phrased like that before. To him *it was as if an orchestra was behind it*." [Emphasis added. N.H.]

And that reminded me of what happened one night in the early 1930's, when a delegation of top brass from the Boston Symphony Orchestra—all of them unfamiliar with jazz but brought there by rumor of genius—stood in Louis Armstrong's dressing room and asked him to play a passage they had heard in his act. Louis picked up his horn and obliged, performing the requested passage and then improvising a dazzling stream of variations.

Shaking their heads, these "legitimate" trumpet players left the room, one of them saying, "I watched his fingers and I still don't know how he does it. I also don't know how it is that, playing there all by himself, he sounded as if a whole orchestra were behind him. I never heard a musician like this, and I thought he was just a colored entertainer."

But during the previous decade, in a series of deeply influential recordings, Louis had already shown to all who would listen that he was the first toweringly creative soloist in jazz. He did not create jazz, as André Hodeir, the French critic, has claimed; but Louis in the 1920's did transcend and extend the beginnings of jazz in collective improvisation. As Gunther Schuller has observed in his book, *Early Jazz* (Oxford University Press), Louis established "the general stylistic direction of jazz for several decades to come." Schuller was writing in particular about a 1928 recording, *West End Blues*, in which, he asserts, Armstrong served notice that "jazz could never again revert to being solely an entertainment or folk music. . . .[Jazz now] had the potential capacity to compete with the highest order of previously known musical expression."

Except for true jazz believers in his own country and throughout the world, this concept of Louis Armstrong as a most serious, stunningly innovative artist is unfamiliar. During the last forty years of his life, most of Armstrong's audiences saw Louis as an entertainer—his hands stretched out wide, in one of them a trumpet and a large, white handkerchief, and on his face the broadest and seemingly most durable grin in the history of Western man. He was often seen in the movies and on prime-time television variety shows, and he had a number of hit records, but he was by no means held in awe by the general public. Yet this was the man who had changed the very shape of jazz as fundamentally and permanently as Beethoven had changed the shape of the symphony.

But the musicians knew. In Chicago, when they came to marvel—and try to steal some secrets—as Louis played with King Oliver. And then, in 1924, when Louis at the age of twenty-four made his first appearance in New York, the musicians there also knew. Louis had come to play with Fletcher Henderson's big band. There were no jazz critics then. Nobody but the musicians took the music seriously, so they are our only historians. Rex Stewart, long before he himself became an international force with Duke Ellington's orchestra, remembered: "We had never heard anybody improvise that way—the brilliance and boldness of his ideas, the fantastic way he developed them, the deepness of his swing, and that gloriously full, clear sound. It was stunning! I went mad with the rest of the musicians. I tried to walk like him, talk like him, eat like him, sleep like him. I even bought a pair of big policeman shoes like he used to wear and I stood outside his apartment waiting for him to come out so I could look at him."

Before Louis Armstrong came to his blazing maturity in the 1920's, there had, of course, been other notable jazz soloists. Some, like Buddy Bolden in New Orleans, are forever misted in legend because they never recorded. Others, like King Joe Oliver and players in Chicago, New York, and the Southwest were often forcefully, pungently distinctive. But none had the sweep, the extended melodic imagination, and the rhythmic inventiveness of Louis. None could make simplicity so profound or high-register fireworks so dramatically cohesive. And none, above all, had ever before so dominated the jazz ensemble, whether small combo or big band. The first fully liberated jazz soloist, Armstrong hugely influenced soloists on all instruments, and he helped free all who followed. They were still part of a collectively swinging group, but they had a lot more space in which to stretch out for themselves.

Gunther Schuller, an instrumentalist and a composer, emphasized in *Early Jazz* the four salient elements which set Louis apart from all the jazz musicians who had preceded him: ". . . (1) his superior choice of notes and the resultant shape of his lines; (2) his incomparable basic quality of tone; (3) his equally incomparable sense of swing, that is, the sureness with which notes are placed in the time continuum and the remarkably varied attack and release properties of his phrasing; (4) and, perhaps his most individualistic contribution, the subtly varied repertory of vibratos and shakes with which Armstrong colors and embellishes individual notes. The importance of the last fact cannot be emphasized enough, since it gives an Armstrong solo that peculiar sense of inner drive and forward momentum. Armstrong was incapable of not swinging."

Back in New Orleans, when he was still a boy—who had learned to play trumpet in a waifs' home where he had been sequestered for celebrating New Year's Eve by shooting off a gun—Louis had already shown unmistakable signs that he was becoming a soloist unlike any New Orleans had ever heard or even imagined. Trumpeter Mutt Carey, known as the "Blues King of New Orleans" when Louis was a lad, once let the teenager take his chair in Kid Ory's band, one of the city's most crisply proficient combos.

"That Louis," Carey recalled, "played more blues

than I ever heard in my life. It never had struck my mind the blues could be interpreted so many different ways. Every time he played a chorus it was different, and yet you knew it was the blues."

On that day Mutt abdicated as the city's blues king.

Almost from the first time he picked up a horn, Louis has exemplified Duke Ellington's dictum, "Nobody is as serious about music as a jazz musician is serious about music."

"When I pick up that horn," Louis, at sixty, told Gilbert Millstein, "that's all. The world's behind me, and I don't concentrate on nothing but that horn. I mean I don't feel no different about that horn now than I did when I was playing in New Orleans. No, that's my living and my life. I love them notes. That's why I try to make them right. Any part of the day, you're liable to see me doing something toward [playing] that night. . . . I don't want a million dollars. See what I mean? There's no medals. I mean, you got to live with that horn. That's why I married four times. The chicks didn't live with that horn. If they had, they would figure out, 'Why should I get him all upset and get to fighting and hit him in the chops, it's liable to hurt him?'"

And because music was the consuming passion, obsession, and pride of his life, Louis took care of himself so that he would always be in condition, so that younger players like Dizzy Gillespie could marvel at what Dizzy called Louis's "phenomenal chops." And in the years of his ascent he had to be in condition for jam sessions.

Many of those sessions were cooperative rather than competitive. As Louis once said of after-hours improvising with Bix Beiderbecke in Chicago in the late 1920's: "Everybody was feeling each other's note or chord, blending with each other instead of trying to cut each other."

There were times, however, when these were martial sessions. As when, also in the 1920's, Johnny Dunn, the top trumpet-gun in New York, confronted Louis at the Dreamland in Chicago. They traded choruses for a while, Louis playing with his eyes closed. "All of a sudden," Armstrong recalled, "I didn't hear anything. Johnny Dunn had just *eased* away."

It was so hard to cut Louis in a session, not only because of his soaring inventiveness, but also because of the extraordinary power with which he played. Critic Ralph Gleason once quoted Louis as telling of how he had sat in one night with Count Basie's band in Florida. "I was just having fun," said Louis, "and Count said to me, 'Damn! I ain't never heard that much strong horn played in all my life!' Now, Count Basie's trumpet players are all good musicians," Louis continued, "but they run away from their notes. Why? Because they don't keep their lips fortified."

It also took a lot of self-fortification for Louis to keep on coping with the Jim Crow that was an obbligato to his life. For many, many years, famed as he was in Europe, when he'd go on the road in his own country, only certain places, black places, would house and feed Louis and his band. All black jazz musicians, no matter how lauded for their contributions to America's "indigenous art form," were pariahs on the road until comparatively recent times. A member of the Count Basie band, which had just come off the road in the early 1950's, told me: "Can you imagine what it feels like to begin pulling up to a gas station and see the attendant running like the hell to lock the men's room. No, you can't imagine it."

In Louis Armstrong's life one of many pungent illustrations of that dimension of the black experience took place in 1931, when Louis, having triumphed in New York and Chicago, returned to his home town which was waiting to pay tribute. There were crowds and banners and a week's engagement at a prestigious club where no black band had ever played. On opening night Louis waited for the radio announcer to start the club's regular broadcast, but the latter could not bring himself, as he said within Louis's hearing, to "announce that nigger man." Turning to his musicians Louis asked for a resounding chord and proceeded to announce the show himself. "It was the first time," Louis said to his first biographer, the Belgian, Robert Goffin, that "a Negro *spoke* on the radio down there."

Twenty-six years later, when Louis Armstrong had long since been comfortably established in the public mind as a most genial and wholly uncontroversial minstrel, millions of Americans were shocked at Armstrong's reaction when Governor Orville Faubus of Arkansas mightily resisted school integration in that state, the Supreme Court notwithstanding, while President Eisenhower temporized. "The way they are treating my people in the South," Louis told the press, "the government can go to hell!" As for the widely beloved Ike, Louis observed, "The President has no guts."

In 1965, as Ralph Gleason has reported, when Martin Luther King's march on Selma, Alabama, was brutally attacked by local and state constabulary, Louis Armstrong, then in Copenhagen, said after watching the carnage on television, "They would beat Jesus if he was black and marched."

For black musicians who had come up with Louis in the 1920's and '30's, this nongrinning Louis "Satchmo" Armstrong was no surprise. "If he had been grinning all the time *inside* all those years," one of his old sidemen said, "how would he have been able to play the blues the way he does?"

Yet most of Louis's onstage high spirits were not feigned. He greatly enjoyed entertaining, getting through, pleasing an audience. And he certainly enjoyed the act of music. For him playing was a celebration of that act and he often celebrated it with wit. "A lot of people underestimate Louis's *musical* sense of humor," Dizzy Gillespie once said. "Many times, listening, I used to laugh right in the middle of his solos."

Because Louis Armstrong was so much the entertainer from the 1930's on, there were some who maintained that Louis had stopped being a vital musician. But, as Martin Williams has observed in *The Jazz Tradition:*

"Well into his sixties, Armstrong would play on some evenings in an astonishing way—astonishing not so much because of what he played as that he played it with such power, sureness, firmness, authority, such commanding presence as to be beyond category, almost (as they say of Beethoven's late quartets) to be beyond music. When he played this way, matters of style, other jazzmen, and most other musicians simply drop away as we hear his eloquence. The show biz personality act, the coasting, the forced jokes and sometimes forced geniality, the emotional tenor of much of Armstrong's music past and present (that of a marvelously exuberant but complex child)—all these drop away and we hear a surpassing artist create for us, each of us, a surpassing art."

Or as clarinetist Edmond Hall, who was with Louis on the road for a long time during Armstrong's "entertaining" years, once said, "There'd be times when, even on a number I'd heard so often, Louis's sound would just get *cracking* and I'd get goose pimples."

Not too long before Louis died, in 1971, a young

trumpet player and I were listening to him in a huge hotel room. Louis had been jiving his way through *Mack the Knife* and then, without an introduction, moved into his old theme, *When It's Sleepy Time Down South*. Staying close to the melody, Louis was subtly adding a new dimension to the song, a chilling and yet exhilarating fusion of poignancy and strength. There were tears in the eyes of the musician standing next to me. "Man," he said, "Pops makes you feel so *good*."

And also of Pops it could be said what he said of King Oliver: "My, what a punch that man had. . . . And could he shout a tune! Ump!"

jazz is:

"You know what annoys the hell out of me?" says **Jimmy Garrison.** The bassist, who has played with John Coltrane, among many other prestigious jazz musicians, stops and shakes his head. "It's when people come up and ask if I ever recorded any serious music."

John Lewis, pianist, former sideman with Lester Young, Dizzy Gillespie, and Charlie Parker, and longtime musical director of the Modern Jazz Quartet, teaching a class in advanced jazz improvisation at Harvard University, is asked by a student, "Can swing be written into a score?"

"No," says Professor Lewis. "Swing is

high musicality. It is like Serkin playing a Beethoven sonata. He knows all the notes, but he also knows what else is there."

Frank Lowe, avant-garde tenor saxophonist, player, as he puts it, of "spontaneous improvisational music," saying: "People still tend to think of this music as something where you have to put on some slick clothes, get high, and go down into some dungeon in order to listen to it. Instead of relaxing, bringing your mother, your kids and going out and having some food and just breathing and relaxing and enjoying the music."

the mainstream generations

Teddy Wilson

Benny Goodman

Three men in tuxedos—a pianist and bassist in their early sixties and a drummer in his late twenties—improvising on *Runnin' Wild*. The pianist, dignified in bearing, his hair and neat mustache graying, shows no discernible emotion as he plays with swift precision, his touch so light that the keys seem barely to go down. Yet each note is being clearly and flowingly knit into an airborne design which keeps building momentum, made all the more exciting by a series of ringing octaves in the right hand that conjure up the image of a full, standing trumpet section playing in unison.

Meanwhile, the other jazz elder, a round, compact man with a huge smile, is laying down a bass line so resilient and firm, and so full in tone, that the whole room appears to pulse to its reverberations. The intent young percussionist, smiling slightly, is making the cymbals dance under his brushes while a sound comes from them like a deep, satisfied breath. Suddenly, switching to sticks, he executes a drum break—bass and piano silent—that hits the room with the shock of a crack of lightning. The trio reunited, applause begins to rise throughout a glistening final chorus. The song finished, the bass player leans over and hugs the drummer. The pianist looks at them and then says into the microphone, "I'd like to introduce my collegues—Milt Hinton on the bass, and I am especially proud to be presenting, on the drums, Ted Wilson."

The pianist is Teddy Wilson.

This is a story of jazz generations; of the cyclical audiences for jazz (especially classic jazz); of an increasing jazz phenomenon that will take clearer and more variegated form for the rest of the century—jazz in the academy. It is yet another indication of how diverse are the origins of jazz fathers and their sons.

Having heard drummer Ted Wilson, I mentioned to his father—the perennially graceful swing-era pianist who presided over many of Billie Holiday's more memorable record sessions—that his son sounds, at times, remarkably like a young Jo Jones in his mastery of brush and cymbal play.

"Yes," Teddy Wilson said, his face actually beaming, a rare sight, "there's a lot of Jo in him, but there's some Gene Krupa, too, and a little of Cozy Cole. When Ted was no more than six or so, I started taking him with me when I had a radio program on CBS Saturday afternoons with Jo and Milt Hinton, and I would also bring him around to the Metropole, that big bar on Seventh Avenue, where Gene Krupa and Cozy Cole often played. Ted is going to be a fine drummer. But he's also continuing his education. He's working for his master's degree in composition at Queens College and for the past few years he's been on the music faculty at Kingsborough Community College in Brooklyn.

"It's a funny thing," Teddy Wilson said of his son. "I've taken him around to hear Max Roach and some of the younger guys who play what's called modern jazz, but Ted still prefers the kind of music I've been part of for so long. At least it's a style that seems to be coming back. More and more people seem to be developing a sense of jazz history and they want to hear as much of the whole spectrum of jazz as they can—old blues singers, people like myself, and the so-called avant-garde. For a while, though, it seemed like a lot of us older players had hardly any audience at all."

For some twenty years, until around 1974, Teddy Wilson's music—part of what critic Stanley Dance has characterized as "mainstream jazz"—had indeed been decidedly unmodish. "Mainstream" can also be called swing-era or classic jazz. By contrast with the rough-and-ready counterpoint of early New Orleans jazz and the robust but choppy music of its white offshoots, Dixieland and the "Chicago jazz" of the 1920's, swing-era musicians had smoothed out the beat. There was no less rhythmic excitement, but the pulse had become more flowing.

In the 1930's there was also more focus on melodic improvisation—from Louis Armstrong, who had begun to influence nearly every soloist, on whatever instrument, in the previous decade, to tenor saxophonist Lester Young, the quintessence of swing-era rhythmic and melodic sophistication. Young served as a highly influential bridge to what became known in the 1940's as "bop," or modern jazz. Since the 1940's the music has become more complex rhythmically; and especially since the frontier-expanding work of the late John Coltrane, its harmonic language has gone beyond chords to tone clusters, diverse fusions of pitches and timbres, and spirals of colors for which there is as yet no harmonic nomenclature.

Although swing-era jazz is more accessible to the nonexpert listener than the forms which succeeded it, this kind of music had until recently fallen out of favor. A nucleus of middle-aged and somewhat older listeners have continued to support as much of it as they have had a chance to hear in clubs and on recordings, but those in the younger generation who are "into music," as they say, had either been captured by rock or, in the case of a minority of hip black and white listeners, had turned to the more or less "free form" jazz of John Coltrane and his successors, most of whom eschew the very term "jazz" and call what they do Black music or just plain music. (This avant-garde way of playing sometimes sounds painfully harsh and directionless to noninitiates and is also marked by a propensity of many of its practitioners to take at least forty minutes to dip into one song.)

During the rather barren decades—the 1950's, '60's, and early '70's—for swing-era jazzmen, Teddy Wilson himself seldom lacked for work. Acting for the most part as his own booking agent, he toured Europe and Japan frequently, while somehow finding all manner of shorter engagements in the United States. Many of his contemporaries, however, have been forced to no longer consider themselves full-time jazz musicians. Veterans of some of the more exciting bands of the swing era—Jimmie Lunceford, Count Basie, Benny Carter— have had to take day jobs as messengers, post-office employes, or schoolteachers while clutching a fragment of the jazz life through whatever music engagements they have been able to get on weekends.

"The climate is changing," Teddy Wilson notes. "In Europe there has always been a greater and deeper interest in all of jazz, including my generation of players, than exists here. But even there, during the past couple of years, I've been getting requests for autographs as if I was back thirty-five years ago with Benny Goodman. The same thing is beginning to happen in America. At a concert I played at the State University at Stony Brook a while ago, I was besieged by people wanting autographs. Not only faculty members but also college and high-school students, and even elementary-school kids. That would have been unheard of a few years ago."

It is Teddy Wilson's thesis that this regeneration of interest in classic jazz indicates that many young people are growing out of rock. "What we play," he explains, "is absolutely new to so many listeners whose tastes have been formed by the Beatles and groups like that since the early nineteen-sixties. We got hardly any air play during all those years, so it's as if they have just discovered us. Furthermore, I do believe that any youngster who is genuinely interested in music eventually has to leave much of rock behind. I don't want to sound immodest, but what musicians like myself play is like Ph.D. music compared to the nursery-school sounds of a lot of rock and roll. They've *got* to grow out of it. And that goes for their parents, too. I mean the kind of parents who try to pretend they love rock so their kids won't think they're old fogies. You can only maintain that stance so long—unless, in musical terms, you're retarded."

Ted Wilson reports similar findings. A thin, serious but not somber young man, the sometime drummer in his father's trio strongly resembles pictures of jazz classicist Teddy Wilson taken in the 1930's. Among other responsibilities at Kingsborough Community college, the younger Wilson teaches courses in the history of music. While covering the forms of European composition and performance from Gregorian chants to contemporary classical directions, he draws parallels between those forms and jazz—the emphasis on counterpoint in some baroque music, for instance, as compared with that in Dixieland jazz. And the ways in which both Sergei Prokofiev and Duke Ellington have transmuted classical forms with modern harmonic concepts.

"What's especially interesting," Ted Wilson observes, "is the students' reactions when we begin to really explore jazz. When I play them recordings by King Joe Oliver with Louis Armstrong, the Benny Goodman Quartet, and Duke, everybody flips out. In one of my classes I had forty-two students, but when we went into jazz there were over a hundred people jammed into that room a few days later. It's all brand new to them. They haven't heard it on the radio, but once they're really exposed to classic jazz they begin to connect with it."

It is Ted Wilson's opinion that his students do not know that he is the son of the Teddy Wilson whose work he analyzes during the course in music history. A stubbornly independent young man, he is almost obsessed with the desire not to trade on his father's name. "I think that one of the reasons I didn't become a pianist," Ted Wilson says, "is that when I started piano lessons around the age of seven, it was like a pattern had been laid out for me. I was going to follow in my father's footsteps. Well, I wasn't going to do that." Another index of the younger Wilson's obstinacy was his decision, when his parents were divorced, that although he was only ten at the time, he—not any court paper—would determine which parent he would live with and for how long at a time.

In any case, the relationship between the Kingsborough Community College lecturer and Jazz Personage Teddy Wilson is never mentioned in class. "When we come to the Benny Goodman Quartet," Ted Wilson emphasizes, "I just say the pianist is Teddy Wilson. There is Teddy Wilson the musician, and Teddy Wilson the father. My responsibility is to tell them about the musician. I do explain, of course, how he held that group together. For instance, when he's playing behind Lionel Hampton on a recording, I have them listen to the bass lines Teddy Wilson is playing and I point out the power and swing they add to the group as a whole. And if the class is ready for it, I analyze why Teddy Wilson has been such an influential jazz pianist.

"My father's big hero," Ted Wilson continues, "was Art Tatum. The man had incredible technique; there was virtually nothing he couldn't do on the piano. But Tatum was essentially a solo pianist, not a rhythm-section player. Fats Waller and Count Basie, on the other hand, were rhythm-section pianists, but they didn't have Teddy Wilson's sense of inner voices. He always had a definite, clear melodic line going on top and a powerful but controlled rhythm line on the bottom. Between top and bottom, however, there was so much going on—harmonic colorations and continually inventive countermelodies. In one sense, the essence of what he was doing was contrapuntal, but those inner voices never detracted from the principal melody or got in the way of the swinging. When my father's in a group it's always like having two piano players in one.

"He's a key figure in the evolution of jazz," the music historian says of his father. "He came out of Earl Hines and Fats Waller and Art Tatum, but then he developed a distinctive style of his own that helped shape a whole school of rhythmically and harmonically sophisticated, lyrical pianists from the 1940's on—musicians such as Hank Jones, Jimmy Rowles. Tommy Flanagan, Dick Katz, the late Richie Powell, and Bud Powell, to a certain extent. I mean Teddy Wilson was a pioneer."

A few days after my conversation with the assistant professor of music, I went to a recording session at which the pioneer was to record, without accompaniment, an album of Fats Waller compositions. The site was Warp Studios in the West Village, near the Hudson River. The atmosphere is uncommonly relaxed—bold, cheerful paintings, various irreverent posters and news clips, leather chairs, a couch, and a young, tieless engineer, Fred Miller, who wears his hair in a long ponytail. The a&r man* was Stanley Dance, who speaks somewhat like an amiable English country squire, but who has long and deep roots in this country. A confidante of Duke Ellington, among many other jazz musicians, Dance is naturally low key, given to mild suggestions rather than authorita-

*The a&r (artists and repertory) man is the studio official who is in charge of a recording session.

rian pronouncements.

Teddy Wilson, who is never late for a date, was already on hand when I arrived. Dressed in a dark blue suit and a pink-and-blue figured tie, Wilson, wearing glasses, was looking over some manuscript paper. I should note here, because it is unusual in my years of hanging out at jazz-record sessions, that throughout the Waller date Wilson kept his suit jacket on and never even loosened his tie. By contrast, every other session I've attended has been characterized by the highly informal attire of the musicians, with Duke Ellington's seminars the most beguilingly unpredictable in this respect.

"Oh, he's calm," Teddy Wilson's son had told me. "He's the calmest piano player around. You'll never see him *look* excited. When he *is* excited it comes out in the music. It starts getting fiery and he's likely to break out into a stride piano passage—you know, that James P. Johnson-Fats Waller way of striding across the keyboard, alternating single notes and chords with your left hand, with your right hand going fast and strong. And, of course, he always wears a suit and tie. He's like a college professor."

For the Waller date, Teddy Wilson had been working on some tunes on the six-foot, one-inch Japanese Yamaha piano he keeps at home in Hillsdale, New Jersey, where he lives with his third wife, Joan (pronounced Jo-Ann), their two small children, and her son by a previous marriage whom Wilson has adopted. (All three youngsters are musical, as is Steven Wilson, the son of an earlier Wilson marriage, who has studied drums in Paris with master jazz teacher Kenny "Klook" Clarke.)

Stanley Dance had also brought in some Waller tunes for the session, including several that had never been recorded before—even by that burner-of-the-candle-at-both-ends himself. Wilson tried out the Steinway in the studio for a few minutes, nodded his head affirmatively, and went on to produce a flawless take of *Black and Blue*. Coming into the control room he sat on a stool and, his right hand on his cheek, listened intently to the performance as Dance laughed appreciatively at a number of particularly subtle improvisatory turns. Wilson approved the take, returned to the studio, and went into an ebulliently swinging version of *Stealin' Apples*. This take too was perfectly proportioned and continually flowing, as if Wilson had been playing nothing else for a month.

"Let's go on through the rest," Wilson told Dance. "We can always come back and do another take if we want to polish up some of them."

Finally proving that even he could err musically, Wilson hit a clam during the first few bars of *I've Got A Feeling I'm Falling*, but then, on the second take, he sailed through a lovely, long-lined, ruminative introduction after which he set the tune on fire in a series of organically developed climaxes which had Dance chuckling in pleasure and the engineer tapping his feet. Wilson's own expression was impassive.

"It all sounds private somehow, doesn't it?" Stanley Dance said as Wilson moved into *My Fate Is In Your Hands*. He looked at Teddy through the window. "It's like a session in someone's living room at two in the morning."

During a break the pianist used the telephone to check on a club engagement the following week. Before the music resumed I asked him if, after all these years of night-club playing and concerts and record sessions, he ever got bored.

"Oh," Teddy Wilson said, "at some point some night my interest may flag a little. But my cure for that is to change the tempo or change the song writer. I might decide to reach back and play Irving Berlin's *Remember*, or go into Thelonious Monk's *'Round About Midnight*. One way or another I can always make it interesting again. Even if I'm not feeling well—a cold or something—once I start playing for a few minutes the music starts taking off."

He looked at his engagement book again, filling in a date. "This really is a wonderful way to make a living out of a hobby. I can play the piano for $1,000 a night or I can play all night for nothing, which is what I could do if I retired. But like Duke says, 'Retire to what?' Same thing with traveling. If I were rich I'd go to Stockholm, the Far East, Latin America. This way, I get paid to go to those places. And whever I go—Tokyo, Rome, Copenhagen—it's old-home week. I get together with musicians I've played with there before, and wherever it is there are people in the audience who know my music, everything I've recorded, almost better than I do."

There was a time, early in Wilson's life, during which it appeared that he might move in another direction—taking the route that led his father, James Augustus Wilson, to become head of the English department at Tuskegee Institute in Alabama and his mother, Pearl Shaw Wilson (Teddy's middle name is Shaw) to become expert in teaching reading and writing to adults and later to function as chief librarian at Tuskegee.

Born in Austin, Texas, on November 24, 1912, Teddy was six when his family moved to Tuskegee, where he grew up. At home, in addition to recordings by Caruso and John McCormack, there were also blues sides by Trixie Smith and Mamie Smith, and Tuskegee being a boarding school there were the students' record collections—the sides most memorable for Teddy having been Fats Waller's *Handful of*

Keys, Louis Armstrong's *West End Blues* with Earl Hines, and the Bix Beiderbecke-Frank Trumbauer *Singin' the Blues.* There were also summer vacations in Detroit—where one of his mother's sisters lived—when the boy heard and marveled at the touring jazz bands, among them Fletcher Henderson and McKinney's Cotton Pickers.

Yet dutifully he continued going to school, finally making an agreement with his mother that he'd try a year of majoring in music theory at Talladega College in Alabama. "It didn't take," Teddy Wilson laughs in recollection. "After a taste of the night music of Detroit and Chicago, I thought that people who wanted to be doctors or teachers of schoolteachers didn't know what they were missing."

With his mother's approval, and to her subsequent pride, Wilson left school after a year to become a professional jazzman, settling for a time in Detroit and then Toledo. He was befriended by Art Tatum. "That man," says Wilson, "had the most phenomenal musical gifts I've ever heard. He was miraculous. It was like someone hitting a home run every time he picks up a bat. We became such fast friends that I was allowed to interrupt him anytime he was playing at the house parties in Toledo we used to make every night. When I asked him, he would stop and replay a passage very slowly, showing me the fingering on some of those runs of his. You just couldn't figure them out by ear at the tempo he played them."

Teddy Wilson came to New York because John Hammond, a young jazz enthusiast and a&r man, listened to the radio whenever he traveled. One night in 1933, Clarence Moore's band was substituting for Earl Hines's orchestra at the Grand Terrace in Chicago, and Hammond, turning the dial, heard a remarkably inventive pianist in Moore's group. Acting instantly, as usual, to satisfy his musical curiosity,

Hammond called the radio station and was informed that the name of the musician in question was Teddy Wilson.

At the time, Benny Carter, an extraordinarily resourceful alto saxophonist and arranger, was struggling to keep his band alive in New York, a particularly urgent need being an enlivening pianist. Hammond, a friend of Carter, told him of his discovery and advanced Carter the money to go to Chicago to recruit the young pianist.

"When I got to New York," Wilson remembers, "I learned an awful lot from Benny Carter, and Red Norvo was also very good to me, hiring me for record dates behind his wife, Mildred Bailey." Particularly important to Wilson's seasoning had been three months on the road at the beginning of 1933 with Louis Armstrong's big band. "It was a privilege to hear that man play every night," Wilson says. "He was such a master of melodic improvisation, and he never hit a note that didn't have a great deal of meaning. Every note was pure music."

In New York John Hammond secured a number of record dates, including sessions he himself directed, for Teddy Wilson, and it was Hammond who persuaded Brunswick to launch the now-classic Billie Holiday small-combo sessions with Teddy Wilson in charge.

"Those sessions were sheer joy," Wilson says. "I had never heard a girl with a sound like Billie's. She could just say 'Hello' or 'Good morning' and it was a musical experience. And her singing, in a very integral way, was a reflection of her whole psychology, her experience. What you heard when she sang was the very essence of her character. And the musicians on those sessions were the cream of the big bands. When Duke was in town, I'd call Johnny Hodges and Harry Carney. When Basie came through, we'd use Buck Clayton and Lester

Young. You could never have gotten a collection of musicians like that together in public, but they did these record dates, for something like $20 a three-hour session, for their own pleasure. And since everyone knew he was playing with the best there was, everyone on the date stimulated everybody else. That's why those records stand up so well forty years later. And Billie—well, we didn't get the top pick of the tunes, those were for the big dance bands with radio time; but she would often just sing her own melody and it would be better than what the song writer had come up with."

It was John Hammond, too, who had persuaded Benny Goodman—and it took a lot of persuasion—to hire Teddy Wilson as part of the Benny Goodman Trio (with Gene Krupa) which toured with the Benny Goodman big band. It was the first interracial group of the swing era to perform in public.

"There had been a lot of interracial record sessions," Teddy Wilson observes. "But this—playing in public with Benny—was a breakthrough. I knew of the pressures that were pulling Benny the other way. Guys in the music business were telling him he'd ruin his career if he hired me. They weren't necessarily antiblack; they were businessmen."

From the very beginning of Teddy Wilson's public association with Benny Goodman in 1936 the businessmen were proved wrong. Goodman's career flourished and he went on to add Lionel Hampton, Charlie Christian, and later Cootie Williams, as other big bands also integrated their ranks.

Teddy Wilson left Goodman in 1939 to form a first-rate but short-lived big band of his own. "We failed," Wilson explains, "because M.C.A. [Music Corporation of America] just wasn't behind us. I don't know why. It's a regret of mine. I was really getting interested in writing when I had that band,

and ever since I kind of envied Duke who could always hear the music he wrote in the morning played by a marvelous band that night."

In the years since, Wilson has headed sextets, trios, and when necessary has gone alone to various parts of the world, where he works with local musicians, many of whom he has come to admire a great deal. Wherever he is, whenever he can, his avocation is listening to other piano players.

"The jazz scene still excites me," Wilson says. "The one thing I do miss are the jam sessions. They used to be so important in the development of the great stars of the past. Certain places were known for piano sessions and others as rehearsal grounds for horns. Many times, when I was playing Cafe Society in New York in the early nineteen-forties, I'd go uptown when we closed at four. It was quite a sight, day breaking and a line of musicians waiting to get inside Monroe's Uptown Club just to play. For nothing. Billie Holiday would be singing, Charlie Parker would be playing, for nothing but pleasure.

"Still," Teddy Wilson was saying at the end of the Fats Waller recording session at Warp Studios, "there's so much to listen to these days, I can never catch up. I've yet to hear Cecil Taylor, for example. And I used to try to keep up with classical pianists, too. I had a fine collection at one time. It went back to preelectric recordings: Rachmaninoff playing Chopin, Josef Hofmann, that sort of thing. I managed to keep up with the classical pianists through the advent of Daniel Barenboim, Vladimir Ashkenazy and André Watts, but I haven't had a chance yet to hear those who've come up more recently. I used to play a lot of classical music myself—just at home—but it seemed to me that jazz was where I had a contribution to make. And it is gratifying to hear pianists around the world playing some of the things I've done. Do you know that Art Tatum used a few patterns he might have first heard in my work? It made me feel so good that a man of his ability had found something of mine he'd want to use."

One night, toward the end of one of the Teddy Wilson Trio's engagements at Michael's Pub, the musicians were so involved in a Duke Ellington medley that they seemed entirely oblivious to the table talk and the occasional sounds of high hilarity from the bar outside the room. *Sophisticated Lady* ended in an intricate but flowing interweaving of improvisatory skills and controlled passion which added a dimension to that Ellington standard I had never heard before. Somehow the room became silent, even at the more bibulous tables. The song finished, Teddy Wilson turned around to Milt Hinton and to Ted Wilson, who had played the whole number with brushes gentling his cymbals, and said softly: "That was very good. Very good."

jazz is:

John Coltrane, trying to put the jazz experience in words: "When you're playing with someone who really has something to say, even though they may otherwise be quite different in style, there's one thing that remains constant. And that is the tension of the experience, that electricity, that kind of feeling that is a *lift* sort of feeling. No matter where it happens, you know when that feeling comes upon you, and it makes you feel happy."

A British interviewer, Les Tomkins, saying to **Cecil Taylor**: "Reviewing a performance of yours once, I used the word 'erotic.' How does that strike you?"

   Taylor: "Ha! That's a good word. Yes—loving, joyful, celebration!"

Rex Stewart, who was an enthusiastic student of
all of jazz history, speaking of Gerry Mulligan:
"The first time I heard him, I experienced the
same feeling I had when I first heard Louis
Armstrong in the twenties. One night in the Savoy
Ballroom in New York, when Louis was there, I
got so excited I began breaking glasses. Well,
Gerry hits me that way, too. He has soul, and he
plays and talks like a man who enjoys life and
people. I felt a kinship with him right away. If a
man doesn't feel him, he must be dead."

the white mainstreamer

Gerry Mulligan

Johnny Hodges, Coleman Hawkins

When the redoubtable Charles Mingus brought a large orchestra to New York's Philharmonic Hall one winter evening in the early 1970's, there was a rustle of excitement in the audience as the musicians walked onstage because one of the sidemen—unadvertised—had once been an extraordinarily popular leader of a jazz combo, a world-wide phenomenon.

"How the hell is Gerry Mulligan going to fit in with Mingus?" asked a young woman.

"Mulligan can fit in with just about anybody," her companion said. "You never know any more where or when he's going to turn up, but when he does he lights up the place."

Indeed, during that evening the angularly tall, bearded, relaxed, alert baritone saxophonist with red-gold hair not only played with wit, charm, and exuberance but also, when not soloing or involved in the ensemble, was manifestly enjoying the proceedings as a spectator at least as much as anyone in the audience. He grinned approvingly during others' solos, particularly those of Gene Ammons, and all in all did light up the place.

A few weeks later, appearing with Dave Brubeck and Paul Desmond at Carnegie Hall, Mulligan—this time sharing the top billing—was just as persistently enlivening. As John S. Wilson observed in the *New York Times*, this "perennial guest . . . gave the evening its high point."

Through more than a quarter of a century, Mulligan's presence on the jazz scene has been singularly stimulating, and his history tells a great deal about certain key periods of jazz history—notably the "Birth of the Cool" gestalt of the late 1940's—as well as about what can be called the "white mainstreamer." There are other white mainstreamers—Zoot Sims and drummer Mel Lewis, among them—but Mulligan has a special ecumenical role in jazz history, a role all the more worth exploring in the 1970's when his significance tends to be overlooked.

In a way, Gerry Mulligan is the Huck Finn of jazz, sometimes exuberant, sometimes wistful, a perpetual wanderer.

In 1959, when Mulligan had become internationally renowned as the leader of a pianoless quartet, Dave Brubeck said, "When you listen to Gerry, you feel as if you were listening to the past, present, and future of jazz, all in one tune, and yet it's done with such taste and respect that you're not ever aware of a change in idiom. Mulligan gets the old New Orleans two-beat going with a harmonic awareness of advanced jazz, and you feel not that tradition is being broken, but rather that it's being pushed forward."

That encomium was largely true then; but, in the years since, "advanced jazz" has taken on much more far-reaching and turbulent characteristics, so that it can no longer accurately be said that Mulligan's work, by any means, encompasses the *full* scope of the music. What does remain true (and it is a considerable accomplishment) is Paul Desmond's analysis of Mulligan: "In probably no other jazz instrumentalist can you find such a clear progression from Dixieland through swing and into and out of bebop, all on the same record, if not in the same solo."

Or, as George Russell, an advanced jazz composer then and now, said in the late 1950's: "Mulligan is Mr. Mainstream."

Another musician much impressed by Mulligan was Coleman Hawkins, a man it was quite hard to impress. "Gerry," Hawkins told me some years ago with magisterial solemnity, "is full of the spirit."

What may well have particularly intrigued and pleased such older jazzmen as Coleman Hawkins and Rex Stewart was that Mulligan, as long as it was possible, directed his formidable spirit to the preservation of the jam session. For decades those informal, unpredictable, and often interminable meetings of jazz musicians—usually but not exclusively after hours—were not only a source of pleasure but also a testing ground. The jam session was a strenuous prep school for young jazzmen as well as an arena where the established postgraduates could keep themselves in musical condition to withstand the thrust of the continual lines of new challengers. Sometimes a venerable champion was toppled at one of these jousts, and the startling news spread swiftly through the jazz underground. Sessions, of course, were also places where ideas were shared. "Carving" and "cutting" were not always the hot order of business.

However, the hagiology of the jam session nearly always focused on the victors rather than the sharers. When I was thirteen or fourteen, for example, I used to listen to itinerant jazzmen of considerable proficiency but no special fame tell and retell bardic sagas of jazz wars. In those years the odyssey of Coleman Hawkins was most often recounted: how he had invented the jazz tenor in the twenties; how, at each stop on the road with Fletcher Henderson's band, he would be challenged by the leading local horn-slingers; and how, invariably, he would beat them by sheer fertility of imagination, blinding technique, robustness of tone, and all-around power. And how, one night in Kansas City, the swaggering Hawkins found waiting for him a pride of young tenor saxophonists, among them the still only regionally known Ben Webster, Herschel Evans, and Lester Young.

The tournament lasted through the night and into

the middle of the afternoon of the next day. At its close, Hawkins had been defeated by Lester Young, who had prevailed even though his tone was lighter than Hawkins's and even though he preferred floating spareness to fiery technical virtuosity. Lester had triumphed because during that joust he had more to say, more that was fresh to say, more that was his own to say. Those jam sessions were no place for imitators, for hornmen whose next phrase or next chorus could be predicted. No sensible player competed—though many jumped in with no sense at all and were cut down—unless he felt he had come far enough along on his horn to be able to surprise the established gladiators. To be able to throw them off balance with a way of running changes, or phrasing, or playing with the beat—or all three—that made the reigning musicians suddenly fear that their ideas had gone stale, that these challengers somehow knew something they didn't know, something that had never been conceived before.

The very best of the established musicians survived their occasional defeats, accepting the notice that they had to woodshed more, practice more, dare more. And they, like Hawkins, would come back and reestablish, for a time anyway, their hegemony. Nearly always at these sessions, standing on the edge of the combat, would be the very young players, listening intently, trying to figure out when they ought to make their move, fantasizing the overwhelming victory. And at times those fantasies came swingingly true.

Hardly anyone would have predicted that this dramatic institution would ever fall into disuse, but starting in the 1950's most of the younger musicians, having separated themselves into tight, intensely rehearsed units, began to neglect the old joys and hazards of jamming. Meanwhile, as more of the jazz elders found it difficult to retain secure places in the jazz scene—because the newer audiences were focusing on "modern jazz"—they lost some of their own zest for jamming and, besides, the sessions were harder to find as fewer of their peers were working regularly.

Gerry Mulligan, however, had, by the late 1950's become the Johnny Appleseed of jam sessions, using any playing opportunity he could find to get a session going. At one of the Newport Jazz Festival evenings, for instance, he was scheduled to play only once, but he ended up playing half a dozen times, onstage and later at jam sessions and parties, including one given by impressario Norman Granz, that produced the most spontaneous jazz of the Festival. On that occasion Mulligan was, as he often is, the first horn to play. As the earliest arrivals sized up the resources of the bar, the pianist Nat Pierce began noodling around and almost at once Mulligan, who had turned up wearing a red sweater and a red checked shirt, sat down near him and joined in softly. Soon other hornmen were playing, too, and Mulligan stood up and went into his characteristic rocking motion, his long back acting as a vibrantly tensile seesaw. In his devoted, rhythmic swaying Mulligan resembles an orthodox Jew at his prayers.

It was Mulligan, too, who presently organized the horns to back up the soloists with complementary figures. As had happened at many another jam session, Mulligan inexorably took over and in the course of the next few hours he demonstrated clearly that he had the strength to stand up with venerable volcanoes like Hawkins and Eldridge. The same sort of thing had occurred some months earlier, at a jam session that was staged after hours at Eddie Condon's club, then in Greenwich Village. Francoise Sagan was the guest of honor, and some *Collier's* photographers came, too, to catch her in the process of enjoying native American *musique engagée*. An observer, the magazine writer Richard Gehman, recalled, "It was an unlikely concoction. There were some of Eddie's Dixieland guys, including Wild Bill Davison on trumpet, and there was Zutty Singleton, the New Orleans drummer, and then, representing modern, there were Mulligan and his trombonist, Bob Brookmeyer. Before anyone knew quite what was happening, Mulligan was in charge. Even Wild Bill was following him." Aside from the force of his personality, probably the chief reason Mulligan almost invariably becomes the director of any group, organized or casual, that he is playing with is that he doesn't have to waste time checking his bearings. He has a thorough knowledge and understanding of almost all the idioms in the language of jazz up to and including the Charlie Parker era but ending at the point of John Coltrane.

Jazz has been succinctly defined by its once-preeminent don, the late Marshall Stearns, as "a semi-improvisational American music distinguished by an immediacy of communication, an expressiveness characteristic of the free use of the human voice, and a complex flowing rhythm." Unlike the classical musicians of the time, with their "legitimate" tone and "proper" fingering, the early horn players of New Orleans and other points of jazz orientation used their instruments very much in their own way, ignoring traditional restraints and incorporating the slurs, glissandi, and personal vibrato of speech. Most jazz combinations were small, and the emphasis was on improvisation—often multilinear collective improvisation. Pulsating beneath, through, and over everything else was the beat, polyrhythmic but inclined, at any rate in the rhythm sections, to be heavy and jagged.

Later on, in the twenties and thirties, emphasis on collective improvisation waned, and the soloists, with Louis

Armstrong leading the way, dominated the jazz scene. Large bands emerged, which gave space to the improvising soloist but enclosed him in section work. Meanwhile, the rhythms of jazz were gradually smoothed as some bands, particularly Count Basie's, in the words of one critic, "put wheels on all four beats in the bar."

By the start of the forties, in the view of the restive young jazz musician, the whole situation had become firmly stabilized; nothing new seemed to be happening and there were stirrings of rebellion. Among the rebels were Charlie "Bird" Parker, Dizzy Gillespie, and Thelonious Monk. What they and others did was to widen the harmonic base for jazz improvisation more challengingly than ever before and to make the play of rhythms over the steady meter that is jazz more intricate and subtle than ever before. So challenging and intricate was their work that for a time it took a thoroughly oriented ear to appreciate, or even to follow, the involuted contours of the music's melodic content. The new music was given a variety of names, but the one that has survived most persistently is "modern jazz."

There was one feature of the older jazz that the insurgents did not dispense with—the tradition of the solo. The best of the influential modern jazzmen were so intent on testing and developing their own voices in this new idiom that they preferred to function mainly as soloists whom other musicians played *for*, rather than *with*. Inevitably, a counter-revolution set in, and this was symbolized, and to a large extent touched off by, a series of recordings made by Miles Davis in 1949 and 1950 w th an ensemble of nine instruments. These records were comparable in their impact on a new generation of jazz musicians to the Louis Armstrong Hot Five and Hot Seven records of the 1920's, some of the Duke Ellington and Basie records of the thirties, and the records made by Parker and his associates in the early and middle forties. The counterrevolutionary aspect of the Davis discs was that they again put the stress on ensemble playing. The soloist was still permitted to improvise, but he did so within a cohesive framework of relatively complex, freshly written ensemble material. The rhythmic and harmonic innovations of Parker, Gillespie, and the rest were retained by the new men, but they aimed for a lighter and more flowing rhythmic pulse than had emerged from the guerrilla warfare that had sometimes existed in the early modern-jazz rhythm sections, and a considerably more sensitive and varied dynamic range. Some of the leaping cry and slashing spontaneity of the beginnings of modern jazz were lost, but the records established a standard for coping once again with the problem—solved by the early New Orleans bands for their time, and by Ellington and Basie for theirs—of maintaining each player's individuality and at the same time emphasizing the organized expression of the group.

The Davis records were an arrangers' triumph, and one of the chief arrangers—and the baritone saxophonist—was Gerry Mulligan. In the following years, without in the slightest losing his interest in the jam session, he had continued to concentrate on organized expression. Beginning with a quartet in 1952, he has had a succession of small groups, each of them strongly integrated by means of arrangements and rehearsals but each permitting the soloists to improvise within an airy, if carefully built, structure.

At Newport, the night after Mulligan himself had roared through the free-style jam session at Norman Granz's party, at which soloing was all, or nearly all, one of his quartets—a particularly fine example, at the time, of a modern-jazz group that had chosen the collective approach as the path of its development—performed before an outdoor audience of twelve thousand. Mulligan and Bob Brookmeyer, playing the valve trombone, engaged in loosely contrapuntal conversations, with bass and drums providing the foundation. The colloquy usually began either with both voices stating a theme or with one lining out the melody while the other interpolated comments. As each then soloed, the other continued, but more softly, to contribute supporting, flowing melodic figures that were linked with warm logic to the foreground assertion. The large, tawny, lunging voice of Mulligan's horn contrasted but did not clash with the more burnished, more gently burred singing of Brookmeyer's. Visually, Mulligan was the more commanding of the two. With the bulky baritone saxophone coming down to his knees, seemingly annealed to him, he rocked through each number, sometimes bending halfway over backward in his ardor, while Brookmeyer, also lean and long and slightly hunched over, stood with legs spread apart. The work of the quartet, individually and collectively, was subtle but strong, each voice remaining sensitive to the others not only in the spontaneous interplay of ideas but also in the constantly changing dynamics—from swelling waves of yea-saying to diminuendos so gently whispered that the bass became the loudest voice. The playing was organized with such clarity that all four instruments could be continually followed, and with such balance that, although there had been plenty of opportunity for each horn to release his own feelings, at the close of a number there were no loose ends.

Gerry Mulligan was born on April 6, 1927, in Queens Village, Long Island, the youngest of four brothers. He is three-quarters Irish and a quarter German, and this has led John Lewis, who feels that there have been too few musicians of Irish descent among the major jazz figures, to welcome him into that category with special warmth. Racial references of any kind, however, greatly annoy Mulligan. Some years ago, shortly after an earnest jazz-magazine editor had suggested that most of the best jazz musicians have been blacks, Jews, and Italians, in that order, Mulligan ran into him in a night club and told him fiercely, "The really impressive thing about jazz, and the important musicians like Bird and Miles and me, is that it and we are so individualistic." Mulligan went on to warn the editor not to bring "everything down to some kind of common denominator."

Mulligan grew up in what he feels was a narrow, conventional, and authoritarian Irish Catholic home. He had a driving interest in music before he entered kindergarten, and in the course of a highly peripatetic childhood (his father, a management engineer, was obliged to move about the East Coast and the Middle West) he learned, with almost no formal help, to play the clarinet and various saxophones, as well as to arrange and compose. (Later he also picked up piano, trumpet, and flugelhorn.)

Breaking away from his family in 1944, at the age of seventeen, Mulligan left high school in Philadelphia to take a brief traveling job as an arranger with the Tommy Tucker band. He then had a series of jobs as an arranger or a saxophonist, or both, with various small and large bands, including Claude Thornhill's and Gene Krupa's. However, being sharp-tongued, willful, and intolerant of bad playing, Mulligan had one calamitous run-in after another with his employers.

On one such occasion, while Mulligan was with Gene Krupa, the band had been working and traveling frenetically, and its playing in Mulligan's opinion had become shoddy. One night, at the end of a set, Mulligan rose and, in plain hearing of the audience, upbraided the band in general and then Krupa in particular for his inability or unwillingness to set higher standards. "I told them all to go to hell," Mulligan recalls. At a meeting of the band next day, Krupa lit into the band first, and then into Mulligan for inexcusable behavior in public. Krupa proceeded to fire Mulligan, but he did not hold a grudge against his former employee. "I had to admire that guy," Krupa said a few years later. "You get too much obsequiousness in this business. There was no obsequiousness in him, which I dug."

Meanwhile, along with his lack of obsequiousness, Mulligan was moving ahead rapidly as a musician, mastering the old and new idioms of jazz, and in 1947—in a move that turned out to be vital to his own development and enabled him to become a significant part of jazz history—Mulligan settled down for a time in New York, joining a group of similarly explorative instrumentalists and arrangers in the experiments that led to the Miles Davis *Birth of the Cool* jazz recordings.

In the mid-1940's there were not many places in the United States where modern jazzmen like Charlie Parker and Dizzy Gillespie could find any sort of encouragement: some night clubs on Fifty-second Street and in Harlem, and a few scattered pockets of rebellion in the black sections of other Eastern cities. The rest of the country, in the modern jazzman's view, was a vast, square desert. Not long after an engagement in California, for example, Parker had fled to New York. "Nobody understands our kind of music out on the Coast," he told the critic Leonard Feather. "They *hated* it, Leonard. I can't tell you how I yearned for New York. . . . As I left the Coast, they had a band at Billy Berg's with somebody playing a bass sax and a drummer playing on the temple blocks and ching-

ching-ching cymbals . . . and the people liked it! That was the kind of thing that helped to crack my wig." Even New York was far from perfect, offering little steady work, but it did promise companionship. A musician who was unable to make much of an impression on the outside world could at least tell his story to an audience of his peers, and there were marathon jam sessions, sometimes lasting two or three days, in any apartment that happened to be available, or in a hall when the jazzmen could scrape together the money to hire one. "There was a spirit then," the pianist George Wallington recalls. "We were engrossed in what we were finding out, and we were inspired by each other. Everybody just loved to play. Most of the time we didn't sleep. We'd fall out for an hour or so and go back to playing. It's nothing like that today. Everybody's going out on his own, trying to make a success."

And so it was that Mulligan was drawn to settle in New York. He supported himself largely by writing arrangements for Claude Thornhill's big band and, as he says, he "aced" himself into any jam session he could find. At the sessions there were heads of court who decided whether a newcomer would be admitted or barred, and Mulligan passed all crucial inspections. As an arranger, too, he was making substantial progress, partly because he renewed what had been a slight acquaintance with Gil Evans, the head arranger of the Thornhill band. Evans, then about thirty-five and a stubborn, self-taught pragmatist, had evolved an intricate, richly tapestried personal style, and this had an important influence on Mulligan, among other young musicians.

In 1947 Evans was living in a one-room basement apartment on West 55th Street, behind a Chinese laundry, and that room became the birthplace of at least one major development in modern jazz. Arrangers and instrumentalists went there to play records and talk, and some of the discussions are now regarded as historic. The room and something of what it meant to Mulligan and the others have been described the composer George Russell: "A very big bed took up a lot of the place; there was one big lamp, and a cat named Becky. The linoleum was battered, and there was a little court outside. Inside, it was always very dark. The feeling of the room was timelessness. Whenever you went there, you wouldn't care about conditions outside. You couldn't tell whether it was day or night, summer or winter, and it didn't matter. At all hours, the place was loaded with people who came in and out. Mulligan, though, was there all the time. He was very clever, witty, and saucy, the way he is now. I remember his talking about a musician who was getting a lot of attention by copying another. 'A Sammy Kaye is bad enough,' Gerry said. 'A bastard Sammy Kaye is too much.' Gerry had a chip on his shoulder. He had more or less the same difficulties that made us all bitter and hostile. He was immensely talented, and he didn't have enough of an opportunity to exercise his talent. Gil's influence had a softening effect on him and on all of us. Gil, who loved musical companionship, was the mother hen—the haven in the storm. He was gentle, wise, profound, and extremely perceptive, and he always seemed to have a comforting answer for any kind of problem. He appeared to have no bitterness. As for Gil's musical influence on Gerry, I think that Gerry, with his talent, would have emerged as a major force in jazz anyway. His talent would have surmounted his lack of formal education. But Gil helped. Gil was, and is, one of the strong personalities in written jazz, and I'm sure he influenced all of us. Gerry, however, was better able than any of the rest of us to channel Gil's influences—including the modern classical writers, whose records Gil played—into mainstream jazz.

Gerry was always interested in the way each of us felt about music, but he was impatient with anything that moved too far away from the mainstream."

Out of the turbulence in the Evans apartment grew some extraordinary projects. Evans himself was strongly stimulated by Alban Berg, among other classical composers, and several times he and his friends, each carrying a score, trooped uptown to the Juilliard School of Music to attend rehearsals of Berg compositions. And—what was of far more moment from a jazz point of view—the discussions in the apartment eventually led to the Miles Davis Capitol recordings of 1949-50, which launched what was known throughout the world for years afterward as "cool" jazz. These records stemmed in part from the experience that Evans and Mulligan had had in writing for the Thornhill band, which made use of a wider and more varied range of instrumental colors—French horns and a tuba among them—than any other jazz orchestra of the time. The records also stemmed in part from the daring conceptions of players like Parker, Monk, Gillespie, and the pianist Bud Powell—frontiersmen who had done a good deal of work in small ensembles that relied on improvisation and whose playing was aggressive, challenging, hot, frequently hard, and at tempos that were inclined to be unnerving.

Now Mulligan and Evans felt that they could retain the searching spirit of the frontiersmen but make the music more subtle, more variously colored, and better organized. Discussions began in the apartment about the smallest number of instruments that could express the harmonic range achieved by the Thornhill band. Evans and Mulligan, recruiting other arrangers and instrumentalists as they went along—among them Miles Davis—proceeded to work out the problems involved. Eventually, they decided that the instrumentation should consist of trumpet, trombone, French horn, tuba, alto saxophone, baritone saxophone, piano, bass, and drums. Next the players were recruited, and Davis, whose organizational abilities were vital to the whole project, was installed as the leader. Late in the summer of 1948, after some weeks of rehearsals in hired halls, the new ensemble opened a three-week engagement at the Royal Roost, at Broadway and Forty-seventh Street. Davis insisted that a sign be placed in front of the club reading, "Arrangements by Gerry Mulligan, Gil Evans, and John Lewis"—the first time that any experimental arrangers in jazz, except for Duke Ellington, had ever received billboard credit. At that time the Royal Roost was probably the only night club in the country that would have taken a chance with this new and forbidding type of jazz, and even it failed to extend the Davis group's stay after the first three weeks. The Davis outfit never again appeared in public as a unit, but a few months after the engagement at the Royal Roost the players reassembled at the studios of Capitol Records to make the first of what turned out to be a series of single records that almost immediately intrigued young jazz musicians throughout the country, although most of the critics took longer to catch up, as usual.

In addition to giving currency to a lighter, more flowing beat and a more diversified and subtle dynamic range than had been characteristic of the earlier, more fiery modern jazz, these sessions, in reemphasizing the importance of *collective* interplay, had an influence which in quite diversified ways has lasted into the 1970's. The music's least fruitful influence was on the largely arid, mechanical, almost entirely white "West Coast jazz" of the 1950's (an exception, in terms of musical value, being Mulligan's own quartets of that period). What the West Coast players did not comprehend was that beneath the surface "cool" of the Miles Davis sessions was a great deal of concentrated intensity. At its disciplined core this too was "hot jazz."

By the late 1950's, in direct, angry reaction to the sterile "West Coast jazz" and to the considerable income those white players were receiving from their bowdlerization of authentic jazz, black players in the East began to emphasize "funk," or "soul jazz," a counterthrust most strongly represented by the blues-and-gospel-rooted shouts of combos led by Horace Silver and Art Blakey.

As "soul jazz" took hold and was followed in the 1960's and 1970's by the much more complex but nonetheless aggressively emotional music of John Coltrane, Sonny Rollins, Cecil Taylor, Ornette Coleman, Sam Rivers, Anthony Braxton, the Art Ensemble of Chicago, et al., it appeared in retrospect as if all aspects of "cool jazz" had been transient divagations, the merest footnotes, in jazz history. Actually, this was true of white "West Coast jazz," but not of the Miles Davis Capitol recordings, both with regard to the staying power of that particular music itself, and also in terms of its long-range impact.

Miles Davis, for instance, though he grew much beyond those recordings in subsequent years, was strongly influenced by that search for unprecedentedly variegated combinations of instruments in a small group, by the keen attention to dynamics, and by the need for each player to continually add to the linear and textural designs with more than just accompaniment. So too was the future of John Lewis's (and the Modern Jazz Quartet's) music shaped in part by those sessions. In fact, no one deeply involved—from Max Roach to Lee Konitz—was the same again musically; and each of them in different ways went on to carry what was learned from this experience to other musicians with whom they worked. At its core that experience was a return to—and an expansion of—the concept of jazz as *collective* improvisation. Solos were vital, but in a rich, resonant configuration.

After New York, Mulligan went on to California, wrestled hard and eventually successfully with a heroin habit he had brought west with him, and started the series of softly swinging, contrapuntally improvising quartets which made his international reputation. During those quartet years Mulligan made another significant contribution to jazz—one that is going to return, I expect, with different textures and newer designs. And that is the natural development of contrapuntal swinging. Dave Brubeck had also worked this vein, and while his alto saxophonist Paul Desmond was exceptionally skilled and imaginative in this kind of improvisation, Brubeck too often was plodding. It was Mulligan who made the breakthrough.

As Gunther Schuller noted, when Mulligan's pianoless quartet was a pervasive phenomenon on the jazz scene, "Gerry brought back the contrapuntal way of playing jazz into naked clarity. He has taken away the harmonic background of the piano, which usually veiled multilinear writing for horns in jazz, and he hasn't fallen into the obvious snare of writing classic fugues—of using the classical forms of counterpoint as a basis for his originals and arrangements. His is simply clear linear writing in jazz terms; he has shown that contrapuntal designs can swing. Previous attempts in modern jazz to emphasize polyphonic writing and playing had bogged down, because of the self-conscious stiffness of the players. Where others went out of the jazz field to take forms from classical music and then returned to try to put them into jazz, he has eliminated that step, and thereby eliminated stiffness in multilinear jazz playing. He has also brought humor back into modern jazz. Jazz, which had been so happy a music in the thirties, had become quite serious, and even at times sickly, during the development of the modern idioms. Mulligan has brought back a happy, relaxed feeling, because he is able to relax completely while playing. Sometimes he relaxes too much. But it is this ability to relax that permits him to play with all kinds of groups, in almost any jazz context, and that makes him the big catalyst that he is."

To which Martin Williams added: "The Mulligan groups play *together*, listen to each other, work as a group. . . . Also they get a complexity and density of texture out of their instruments."

There was another kind of impetus Mulligan gave to jazz in the late 1950's and early 1960's and may well—since he is so resilient—contribute again. "Gerry," says Bob Brook-meyer, "has a positive life attitude, in contrast to the suicidal perspective—the Charlie Parker complex—that was prevalent among many post-World War II musicians. Parker was so impressive musically and personally that he set some standards he hadn't meant to. Gerry came as a life-giving current of air to young musicians who had been stifled emotionally and intel-lectually by the idea of death. And in his music he proved that a whisper at times can be more effective and piercing than a shout."

In the 1960's Mulligan also proved his extraordinary capacities as a big-band leader. His orchestra was supple, re-sourceful, the soloists an integral, organic part of the arrange-ments. The band had drive, wit, lyricism, ingenuity—like its leader. But the economics of the jazz scene made it impossible for Mulligan to maintain the band. And so he has continued playing both as incandescent guest and increasingly again as leader. Meanwhile, as more of the older jazz players disappear,

Mulligan remains a particularly important and attractive figure in jazz history for the affection and respect he has shown
jazz elders during long years when few other younger players
did.

One of the remarkable things about the remarkable form of
expression known as jazz, which in the past seventy-five years
has become familiar in the remotest regions of the globe, is
that its collective history has been made by thousands of
fiercely individualistic players. This history has consequently
been a full one, marked by skirmish after skirmish on constantly shifting terrain, yet because it has been so brief, we still
have in our midst survivors of every one of the campaigns. The
eldest of these veterans, who started out working by day as
longshoremen, cigar makers, and the like, and playing jazz by
night—as much for pleasure as for money—are seldom heard
from nowadays, however, except at such invaluable refuges as
Preservation Hall in New Orleans. And the succeeding
generation—professionals from the start, more sophisticated
and more resourceful but no less fiery—have had hard going in
recent decades. In the 1930's most of the best of them played
in large jazz bands of a sort that has almost ceased to exist, and
some of their triumphs are recorded in those hagiological list-
ings called discographies.

 Quite a few of these musicians were sweepingly proficient soloists, able to express through improvisation a range
of ideas and emotions that made many a music student eye his
textbook and teacher with skepticism, and in general they
showed that an organization of perhaps fifteen men could
swing with a drive exhilarating to players and listeners alike.

 In the course of time, though, these musicians gave
way to the first phalanx of what are known as "modern
jazzmen"—somewhat more self-conscious musicians who

worked at expanding or renewing the harmonic and rhythmic language of jazz, and in doing so tended for a time to drop melody into third place. Inevitably, the Jacobins—men like Parker, Gillespie, and Bud Powell—were themselves followed by a generation with even newer ideas. This second phalanx of modern jazzmen, while admiring the sometimes craggy advances of their immediate predecessors and doing their best to consolidate them, felt that it was possible, and agreeable as well, to concentrate on melodic lyricism again, and some of them are still profitably working along that line, though they too have been increasingly challenged by newer, more clangorously venturesome forces.

All these groups, and others, coexist, though their fortunes vary. It is as if Palestrina, Bach, Mozart, Debussy, and Webern were alive at the same time. Many young jazz musicians, however, derive no satisfaction from this extraordinary state of affairs; far from honoring their elders, some of the young in jazz know little about them and care less.

How little they cared was evident one Saturday evening in the summer in 1959 in a large tent at the Timber Grove Club, on Great South Bay, Long Island, when, in the course of a jazz festival, a group of aging musicians met to put on a special kind of revival meeting. The musical director of the festival was Rex Stewart, then middle-aged and performing with Eddie Condon's outfit. He had reassembled as many members of the Fletcher Henderson unit of the 1920's—one of the world's first large jazz bands—as he could, filling the remaining positions with jazzmen of the same era, or a slightly later one. The musicians looked forward to playing together again, especially since the world of jazz had been treating them badly; as a rule, night-club owners, bookers, and record-company executives felt that there was no public for jazz musicians in their forties and fifties, and some members of the reconstituted band were reduced to routine day jobs that had nothing to do with music. Others had jobs with minor rhythm-and-blues bands. A very few—like Coleman Hawkins—had done better, but even they had remained in jazz under less than optimum conditions, artistic or financial.

If a reunion of a great classical group—the Thibaud-Cortot-Casals trio, say—had ever been held at Great South Bay, or anywhere else, young classical musicians would have arrived in swarms. For the Great South Bay Festival, which brought together such eminent jazz musicians as Hawkins, the trombonist J. C. Higginbotham, and the alto saxophonist Hilton Jefferson for the first time in years, only one prominent young jazzman made the two-hour trip out from New York—Gerry Mulligan. Then thirty, Mulligan had already played a decisive part in one of the most recent waves of jazz reform—the wave that had led to a reemphasis on melody and, with it, multilinear collective improvisation. Yet even though he was in the forefront of the innovators at that time, he had continued to listen to and to learn from the older traditionalists. Modern jazz in his view was not a revolution against an *ancien régime* that would be better off buried. He saw it as a natural evolution of the old jazz language, and he had great respect for his musical ancestors.

That Saturday morning Mulligan left his midtown New York apartment and drove out to Great South Bay. He went to listen, but, since he always hopes to find a jam session, he took his saxophone along. When he arrived at the tent a loosely swinging band, led jointly by bassist Bob Haggart and trumpeter Yank Lawson, was performing in a style that might be called swing-era Dixieland. For a moment Mulligan stood listening, and then was visited by a compulsion to play. He picked up his horn and moved up to the bandstand, to the evident satisfaction of the other players. This was the first time Mulligan had ever played with either Lawson or Haggart, but he sounded as if he had rehearsed with their unit for weeks. Meanwhile, Rex Stewart was basking on the beach, resting up for the Fletcher Henderson revival meeting in the evening. Somehow, word reached him that Mulligan had come and was playing, and Stewart, who felt for Mulligan a wholeness of devotion that he extended to few other young jazzmen, hurriedly changed his clothes, ran for his horn, and moved onto the stand. He and Mulligan had never played together, and this was an experience Stewart had been looking forward to for months. The instantaneous, hot rapport between the pair fired all the musicians on the stand into a booting ensemble rideout.

That evening, during the Henderson reunion, there was an extra baritone saxophone in the band. Mulligan had bought a ticket and had filed into the big tent with the rest of the customers. Then he had slipped into the shadows alongside the bandstand, and when the concert of the patriarchs got under way he began playing softly. At a wave from Rex Stewart, Mulligan moved onto the stand, took up a position between Hawkins and J. C. Higginbotham, and played a strong solo. The old-timers seemed pleased to have him there and he was pleased to be there. The last the audience saw of Mulligan, much later that night, he was walking out of the tent into the darkness, still playing.

Around the time of that transgenerational evening at the Great South Bay Jazz Festival, Gerry Mulligan, in an article he had written for *Down Beat*, described a project that had long appealed to him: "I think it would be a good idea to organize a unit composed of some of the older jazzmen and those of the younger musicians who can do it. . . . But first I'd want the group to work out for some time. Then if something of musical value results, we could record it. But I don't like the idea of doing something just to record it. It has to work first."

Except for a few age-mixed bands in New Orleans through the years (usually a fusion of perpetual jazz students from Europe with the native musical aristocracy), there has yet to be a project of the order envisioned by Mulligan. Jazz remains more segregated by age than by any other factor, and that is a great pity and a great loss—to listeners and musicians alike. Nonetheless, the achievement of transgenerational maturity among younger musicians is not beyond possibility; and should such an orchestra finally appear, spanning the decades of jazz, Mulligan is still one of its most likely and logical leaders.

Together with his insistence on paying attention to the whole jazz tradition, Mulligan is also one of the prototypical jazz romantics. He describes, for instance, a small event with large consequences which took place in a small Ohio town when he was in the third grade there. And this brief tale also reflects the boyhood dreams of just about everyone, in any country, who later jumped into the jazz life.

"I was on my way to school," Mulligan recalls, "when I saw the Red Nichols bus sitting in front of a hotel. That moment was probably when I first wanted to become a band musician and go on the road. It was a small old Greyhound bus with a canopied observation platform, and on the bus was printed, 'RED NICHOLS AND HIS FIVE PENNIES.' It all symbolized travel and adventure. I was never the same after that."

jazz is:

A psychiatrist trying to explain the soul-force of
John Coltrane: "It sounds like a man strapped
down and finally screaming to be free."

A symposium on the Cultural and Political
Significance of Charlie Parker at the University of
Massachusetts at Amherst in the spring of 1975.
Black jazz-musician professors speak of the need
for university centers for autonomous black
culture. They also speak fervently of the future of
black music. Silent, on the panel, are two black
musicians, Grachan Moncur III and Jimmy
Garrison. The latter had played with John Coltrane
for a long time. Both musicians have found it hard
in recent years to get work.

     "I don't argue with what you're saying,"
the former John Coltrane sideman finally says,
"but instead of trying to predict where our music is
going, what about coming up with some ideas on
how those of us out there now can get some work?"

Thelonious Monk staring at an interviewer for
Down Beat, and finally saying: "Where's jazz

going? I don't know where it's going. Maybe it's going to hell. You can't make anything go anywhere. It just happens."

Miles Davis telling me some years ago that he was turning down an engagement in a jazz club in Toronto. I asked him why. "Because that motherfucker who owns it told me to fire Philly Joe because he's too *loud*! Nobody can tell me what to do with my music."

Philly Joe Jones, Miles's drummer at the time, was a brilliant, cracklingly aggressive, polyrhythmically swinging mesmerist who often did indeed play loud. "Shee-it," said Miles, "I wouldn't care if he came up on the bandstand in his B.V.D.'s and with one arm, and shouting his head off, just so long as he was there. He's got the fire I want. There's nothing more terrible than playing with a dull rhythm section. Jazz has got to have *that thing*. You have to be born with it. You can't learn it, you can't buy it. You have it or you don't. And no critic can put it into any words. It speaks in the music. It speaks for itself."

miles (alone) ahead

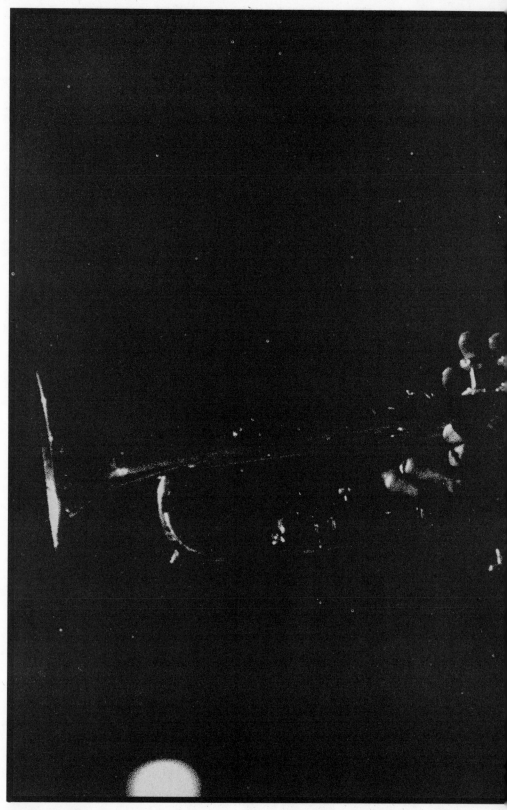

Miles Davis

Philly Joe Jones

"Miles Davis is a leader in jazz," says Gil Evans, "because he has definite confidence in what he likes and he is not *afraid* of what he likes. A lot of other musicians are constantly looking around to hear what the next person is doing and they worry about whether they themselves are in style. Miles has confidence in his own taste, and he goes his own way."

Duke Ellington, in his characteristically expansive way, once likened Miles to Picasso—always changing, always up front somewhere by himself, taking risks, daring others to take risks. I shan't pursue the comparison. I am wary of analogies between creators in different fields. But in jazz Miles Davis has surely been one of the most influentially changeable of all players—the primary designer of "cool jazz," then the leader of the hottest jazz combo since Louis Armstrong's Hot Five, then the orchestrated lyricist of *Sketches of Spain*, and in the 1970's the demonic animator of splinters of electronic sound glistening with rock, jazz, blues, and his own horn of spearing loneliness.

Miles has also been one of the quintessential heroes of the jazz life—a defiant loner, a musician who has tamed bookers, recording-company officials, critics. A dramatic man. Actually, a calculatedly dramatic man, because although he rightly considers himself an artist, a black artist in a white society managed by those hostile or indifferent to both blacks and art, he also knows, as Duke Ellington knew, that he is part of show business.

Since music is commerce as well as art (when it is art), Miles wants and gets his share of material rewards. But since he is also a proud man, he insists he will not dilute his music to get those rewards. So long as he himself has confidence in the validity of each new risk he takes, Miles feels that confidence will extend to his audiences, and so far it has.

"I'm too vain in what I do to play anything really bad musically that I can help not doing," Miles has said. "If I ever feel I *am* getting to the point where I'm playing it safe, I'll stop. That's all I can tell you about how I plan for the future. I'll keep on working until nobody likes me. When I am without an audience, I'll know it before anybody else, and I'll stop."

But Miles is no more likely to stop than Duke Ellington or Louis Armstrong were, than Dizzy Gillespie or Charles Mingus are. And no one can predict what musical turn he will take, or rather invent, next.

I first came to know Miles in the mid-1950's. I had met him several times before, but casually, quickly. And I had heard tales of his forbidding, caustic, blunt temperament. In that respect, if the reports were true, he was again unique. Most jazz musicians are quite accessible. It's difficult, for one thing, to be rigid and uncommunicative and still be in a calling which requires emotional spontaneity above all else. Jazz musicians, moreover, are wanderers by the nature of their trade, and having been so many places they have many stories to tell. And most of them—because they have had so many varied experiences of people and places that sedentary folk can only read about—are unusually perceptive. They are quick and, for the most part, accurate judges of character and motivation. Being among them sharpens the mind and undermines one's own provincial attitudes. And they tend to be generous of spirit.

But watch out for Miles, I was told. A leading booking agent at the time warned me, "He's basically not a nice guy. His conversation, when he bothers to talk to you at all, is made up mainly of insults. That son-of-a-bitch is bad for jazz. He doesn't give a damn for audiences, and he lets them know it by paying no attention to them. I mean you don't have to wave a handkerchief or show your teeth like Louis Armstrong to let the audience feel you care what they think about your music. But not him."

Miles Davis, it turned out, was and is sardonic, impatient with pretentiousness and cant, but also highly intelligent, acutely sensitive to and concerned with audience reactions, and in his personal relationships, inordinately helpful, generous, and, to be sure, mocking. He is also shy.

The only jazz musician I have known who was more shy than Miles was Henry "Red" Allen, the undersung, post-Louis Armstrong New Orleans trumpet player, who came North and presaged a small part of what Miles Davis was later to achieve on trumpet. Red Allen's way of dealing with his shyness was to impersonate a total extrovert on stand, waving his horn, singing, exhorting the audience to drink and drink some more. But off the stand, he was painfully polite, extremely soft-spoken, and so formal that he might have been a most gentle undertaker.

Miles's way of coping with shyness is to affect fierceness. "Like all of us," a musician who has known him for many years explains, "Miles only has a certain amount of energy, and he finds it difficult to meet new people. Rather than subject himself to what is for him a tiring discomfort, he tries to create so forbidding an image of himself that he won't even be bothered."

There is yet another dimension of Miles's wariness and his determination to protect himself emotionally. Coming up in the jazz life—and this has been an inevitable hazard beginning with the music's original conjunction with the purveyors of highly diverse after-dark pleasures—the musician can be exposed to all manner of nocturnal predators: members of organized crime; independent, low-level hustlers; cops on the take; all kinds of grafters, some of them club owners and bookers. (As jazz has increasingly moved into the concert scene the predators are less primitive in their approach.)

A good many musicians have managed to remain reasonably aloof from the more dangerous exploiters and their temptations. Others have become involved, particularly in the 1940's and early 1950's when drug use among jazz musicians was at its height. A picaresque observer of those jazz times was Babs Gonzales, a floating man of uncommon though mysterious resourcefulness who was best known as a singer-composer-satirist, but always appeared to have another unknown, shadowy life—not necessarily an illegal life, so far as I knew, but the kind of survivor's life that kept him away from the overground scene for long periods of unexplained time.

"Miles," Babs Gonzales once told me, "came from a prosperous, upper-middle-class home and was even spoiled a little as a boy. Therefore, there doesn't seem to be any reason for the suspicion he has toward people, right? But he knew some grim times before all this success. For one thing, when he was strung out on heroin—and he's one of the very few who broke the habit all by himself, completely without treatment—Miles was desperate enough to fall in with some pitiless people. Some of them exploited him musically, made him play for very little bread, but he badly needed that little bread. Also, the hoods who ran one jazz club in New York used to beat up on Miles and Bud Powell and other musicians who were strung out and in hock to them. Miles has always been a proud man, and while they didn't break him they hurt him for a long time. Ever since then he's been leery about everybody. With exceptions—and they never know who they'll be."

That Miles came back, entirely on his own, to become a dominant figure in the music, in thrall to no one, is a key element—aside from his musicianship and stubborn originality—in the respect in which he is held by musicians. Once he was in demand again (after a period of decline from the late 1940's until a startlingly lyrical 1955 performance at the Newport Festival), Miles has never let himself be exploited in any way. In this respect he is like Dizzy Gillespie, and unlike Louis Armstrong. Neither Miles nor Dizzy allow white overseers to keep their account books secret from them—a fact that is very strongly held in mind by the succeeding generation of young black musicians who are even more sensitive to white economic domination of the music world than their immediate predecessors.

Miles Davis, in part because of his blistering criticism of decades of white ownership of much of black jazz, has a reputation for being antiwhite. He himself, however, makes the distinction between his scorn for white exploiters (including the political and economic leadership of his country, regardless of political party) and his insistence on measuring each person he knows as an individual, regardless of race.

In terms of music, for instance, as black cultural nationalism was rising among younger musicians, Miles was often criticized for having whites in his band—from Lee Konitz and Bill Evans to various young jazz-rock players in the 1970's. In turn, he said that he had known enough prejudice himself to resist the mandate that he himself should learn how to be prejudiced.

"It's like when I first hired Lee Konitz years ago," Miles recalls. "Some guys said, 'Why do you want an ofay in your band?' I asked them if they knew anybody who could play with a tone like Lee's. If I had to worry about nonsense like that, I wouldn't have a band. I wouldn't care if a cat was green and had red breath—if he could play."

As for the way Miles plays, for all the changes he keeps making in the shapes and textures of his music, he himself continues to be spare (making continually dramatic use of space) and exceptionally incisive in his beat. Few hornmen in the history of jazz have had, for example, as intensifying an effect on a rhythm section—all kinds of rhythm sections. "His conception of time," Cecil Taylor says of Miles, "has led to greater rhythmic freedom for other players. His feeling, for another thing, is so intense that he catapults the drummer, bassist, and pianist together, forcing them to play at the top of their technical ability and forcing them with his own emotional strength to be as emotional as possible."

Miles also has developed an entirely personal sound. In fact, as Gil Evans has observed, "A big part of Miles's creative gift is the creation of sound. He arrived at a time when, because of the innovations of modern jazz, all new players had to find their own sound in relation to the new modes of expression. Miles, for example, couldn't play like Louis Armstrong because that sound would interfere with his thoughts. Miles had to start with almost no sound and then develop one as he went along—a sound suitable for the ideas he wanted to express.

"Finally," Evans continues, "Miles had his own basic sound, which any player must develop. But many players then keep this sound more or less constant. Any variation in their work comes in the actual selection of notes, their harmonic patterns, and their rhythmic usages. Miles, however, is aware of his complete surroundings and takes advantage of the wide range of sound possibilities that exist even in one's own basic sound. He can, in other words, create a particular sound for the existing context. The quality of a certain chord, its tension or lack of tension, can cause him to create a sound appropriate to it. He can put his own substance, his own flesh on a note and then put that note exactly where it belongs."

After Gil Evans made that point, Miles went on to play outside chords and, in the 1970's, he has tended to improvise over pointillistic, continually shifting textures that are given specific gravity as he does indeed put "his own flesh" on those quick fragments of color-in-time.

In all of jazz so far, Miles's horn is perhaps the most subtle delineator of loneliness. A prideful loneliness, to be sure, but no less a chronic condition for all of that. He is, of course, never sentimental, however introspective. Instead, he tends to be, as a French musician once said to me, "insidious, like somebody calling you from the other shore."

As for his musical odyssey (the making of the sound from the other shore), Miles, no more than any other jazz musician, instantly sprang into full-blown individuality (a cliché of the early popular novels and television plays about jazz). Few jazz listeners, in fact, are able, unless they themselves play an instrument with some proficiency, to appreciate how long and hard the jazzman's seasoning is. I mean beyond the initial ability to get around the instrument. First, there is the succession of influences from established players, the absorption of those influences, the struggle to transcend imitation and develop one's own sound and style, and then the testing of what one thinks has been achieved on the ultimate jousting ground of working with the best players in jazz.

The son of a successful dentist and dental surgeon in East St. Louis, Illinois, Miles began playing in school. As soon as he was able to hang out in clubs he listened carefully to local trumpet players, including Clark Terry (later with Duke Ellington and then leader of his own big band). From recordings Miles became variously intrigued with the playing of Roy Eldridge, Harry James, Bobby Hackett, and Buck Clayton.

While Miles was still in high school, the Billy Eckstine band with Charlie Parker and Dizzy Gillespie came to St. Louis. He not only heard Bird and Dizzy but, since the band needed a third trumpet player, played with these fabled hornmen in and around St. Louis for several weeks.

After that experience Miles knew, as have thousands of musicians before and since, that he had to go to New York. Whatever a jazz player's place of origin, New York is still the ultimate jazz academy, and after that the place where jazz reputations are definitively made or broken.

Having enrolled at Juilliard to please his parents, Miles only nominally paid attention to the instructors at that enclave of classical music. Instead he went in search of Charlie Parker, found him, and moved in with him.

"I used to follow Bird around, down to 52nd Street," Miles has recalled. "'Don't be afraid,' he used to tell me. 'Go ahead and play.' Every night on matchbook covers I'd write down chords I'd hear. Everybody helped me. Next day I'd play those chords all day in the practice room at Juilliard, instead of going to classes. Thelonious Monk would write out his chords and tunes for me. Tadd Dameron helped, as did Dizzy, who advised me to study piano, and I did. I finally left Juilliard. I realized I wasn't going to get in any symphony orchestra. And anyway, I had to go down to 52nd Street at night to play with Bird or Coleman Hawkins, so I decided to go that way all the way."

Miles's description of what it was like, as a young player (still very much an apprentice), to work with Charlie

Parker, the most careeningly original musician of the time, is an illumination of the jazz life: "Bird used to play forty different styles. He was never content to remain the same. I remember how at times he would turn the rhythm section around. Like we'd be playing the blues, and Bird would start on the eleventh bar, and as the rhythm section stayed where they were and Bird played where he was, it sounded as if the rhythm section was on one and three instead of two and four. Every time that would happen, Max Roach used to scream at Duke Jordan [the pianist] not to follow Bird, but to stay where he was. Then, eventually, it came around as Bird had planned and we were together again. Bird used to make me play. He'd lead me up on the bandstand. I used to quit every night. The tempos were so fast, the challenge so great. I'd ask, 'What do you need *me* for?'"

Miles Davis's apprenticeship continued. He learned a great deal more about a trumpet's capacity for lyricism from Freddie Webster, who recorded with Sarah Vaughan, among others. "Freddie didn't play a lot of notes," Miles says. "He didn't waste any. I used to try to get his sound. He had a great big tone, like Billy Butterfield, but without a vibrato. Freddie was my best friend. I wanted to play like him. I used to teach him chords, everything I learned at Juilliard. He didn't have the money to go. And in return I'd try to get his tone."

Miles never did get Freddie Webster's tone, but he did learn about lyrical economy from him; and Freddie's lack of vibrato reinforced for Miles what a teacher he'd had in St. Louis once told him. The teacher had been opposed to the pronounced vibrato with which many of the traditional and swing-era jazzmen played, and he warned Miles, "You're gonna get old anyway and start shaking." Accordingly, Miles remembers, "that's how I tried to play. Fast and light—and no vibrato."

By the late 1940's Miles had become established, but for four years, starting in 1949, he was also hooked on heroin. He worked infrequently. When he did work he was rawly inconsistent. Increasingly, he tried not to care about anything, including music. Finally, he exiled himself to Detroit for several months in an attempt to regenerate himself. His fundamental independence having made his addiction insupportable, he holed up in a room for two weeks and, with enormous strength of will, broke the habit. "It was too damn much trouble to keep," he later told me.

Since then Miles has been in command—of himself, and his music, and the conditions he sets for playing it. He keeps on reaching new audiences through continuous changes in his own conception of music, and he keeps on baiting the critics, as when, on his highly successful *Bitches Brew* album, he insisted no personnel or instrumentation be listed.

"You know why I did that?" Miles told a reporter for *Down Beat*. "Because when you give the critics the instrumentation, they know the musicians and they say that he plays this way or he plays like that. So this time they didn't know who was in the band and they had to think for a change."

And he still continues to focus on spontaneity. Reviewing a 1974 Miles Davis concert in the *Washington Post*, Gene Williams wrote that it was as if Miles were leading "his exploring party through a dense electronic rain forest. Sensing a clearing, Davis extends his fingers in a signal and his group halts motionless as a soprano sax or electric guitar or even the leader's trumpet slips ahead alone, reporting what he sees. The leader listens, choosing a path. He arches his body, nodding his head to the desired pulse, beckoning the rhythm guitar, and his group falls in, resuming their journey. Echoing, reverberating, electronically shaped notes and phrases form the strange beautiful foliage and strong life rhythms of Davis's musical world."

Williams made the further point that Miles, customarily, was not directing a rehearsed performance. Instead, "He was literally making [new] music. . . . As a conductor, he is improvising from the kind of form pianist Cecil Taylor was talking about when he said, 'Form is possibility.'"

Miles Davis would have entirely understood what Sidney Bechet, the volcanic soprano saxophonist from New Orleans, meant when he tried, years ago, to tell some of the more rigid jazz traditionalists that this was not music to be preserved under glass. What Bechet said, and Davis exemplifies, was: "There's this mood about the music, a kind of need to be moving. You just can't set it down and hold it. Those Dixieland musicianers, they tried to do that; they tried to write the music down and kind of freeze it. Even when they didn't arrange it to death, they didn't have any place to send it; that's why they lost it. You just can't keep the music unless you move with it."

jazz is:

Drummer **Denzil Best,** remembering **Thelonious Monk** playing the piano when he was a teenager. "People would be calling his changes wrong to his face. If he hadn't been so strong in his mind, he might easily have become discouraged. But he always went his own way and wouldn't change for anything."

Thelonious Monk speaking for himself: "I say play your own way. Don't play what the public wants—you play what you want and let the public pick up what *you* are doing, even if it *does* take them fifteen, twenty years."

Charles Mingus, one night in the late 1950's,
trying out a new piece in a night club, a work of
intricate collective improvisation—an explosion of
cries, instrumental and vocal, of shifting,
undulating rhythms, of wide-ranging dynamics,
from piercing highs to fierce whispers. But the
audience is otherwise distracted, talking, drinking,
laughing at their own jokes. Mingus cuts the music
dead, looks out into the smoke, and says, "If you
think what we're doing is weird, just take a look at
yourselves."

the visions of mingus

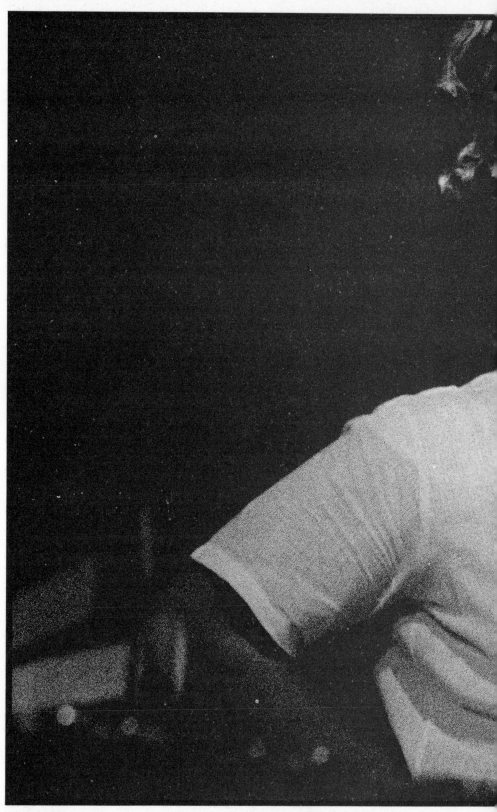

Charles Mingus

Bud Powell

In a fundamental sense, jazz is a history—at its heights—of indomitable individualists. Some have paid heavier dues than others, in part because of temperament, in part because of the particular socio-musical milieu in which they began to shape their own subversive sense of musical order.

Charles Mingus has paid more dues than most, and there was a time when it appeared that the pressures of chronic iconoclasm had finally worn him so far down that whatever music might come from him for the rest of his life would consist of fragmented, attenuated echoes of his boldly, angrily sweeping past.

This lowest point was during the late 1960's. Mingus rarely appeared in public, and when he did his music was almost dispassionately retrospective. In the daytime I'd see him occasionally wandering around the lower East Side, uncommonly subdued, abstracted. The Mingus who had been able to sardonically berate an audience for its careless incivility and then hurl it into the flying center of his musical lightning storms had retreated into himself.

Gone, too, was the Mingus who would call up friends to try out urgent new theories on politics, the dynamics of racial prejudice, the convoluted corruption of the music business—or, without introducing himself or saying anything at all, to play at full volume into the phone the tape of a composition in progress.

"He'll never come back," a longtime musical associate of Mingus said to me while Mingus was in limbo. "He just used himself all up."

I wondered if that could be true and yet, as time went on and Mingus seemed to entirely disappear from the music scene, I still could not believe this protean force had indeed used himself all up. I had seen him rebound before, coming back up from very deep descents into paralyzing self-doubt. On the other hand though, this had turned into his longest period of defeat.

Finally, there *was* news of resurgence—a concert, a new recording. I went to see Mingus in an editing room at Columbia records to savor his return, to find out where he'd been.

Coming toward the door of the editing studio I knew immediately that the regeneration was real. There was strong, thrusting music inside. Mingus music. And as I entered, long, boldly arching Mingus melodies filled the room. A tenor saxophone and a trumpet interwove their improvisatory lines through the swelling, deeply textured designs of a large orchestra whose various sections were also engaged in sinewy interplay. The pulsing beat, as is customary in a Mingus work, changed cadences like speech—gathering momentum in exuberant passages, slowing down for reflection, and sometimes disappearing briefly, leaving a shock of groundlessness.

Mingus, a bearded Buddha in black shirt, white tie, and black pants, puffed at a large, curved pipe as he nodded in approval.

After the music ended I asked Mingus about his time in limbo. "For about three years," he said, "I thought I was finished. Sometimes I couldn't even get out of bed. I wasn't asleep; I just lay there. But living where I do, on East Fifth and Avenue A, deep down on the lower East Side, I began to learn about people, and that started me coming back.

"In that neighborhood," Mingus went on, "they didn't know me from the man in the moon, but they took an interest in me. I'd go into a bar, sit by myself, and I'd hear someone say, 'There's something wrong with this guy. He

doesn't come out of his house for four or five days at a time.'
And they'd invite me to join them. I got to know what friends
are. Ukrainians, blacks, Puerto Ricans—a house painter, a
tailor, a woman who owns a bar, her bartender, a maintenance
man who says, 'I'll walk you home tonight if you get drunk.
And if I get drunk, you walk me home.'

"Sure, in a way it's hell down there. I've been rob-
bed four times. They stole almost everything I had. All that's
left are a Steinway and my basses. So now I've got locks on my
doors, bars on my windows, and a baseball bat near at hand.
But I'm not going to move. Even with the danger. I want to
stay because it's family. We all look out for each other. Not
just against muggers and robbers. There was a time when I
had no money left at all, but the tailor on the block made sure I
had enough to eat."

Mingus, who had always proclaimed the essential,
transcendent humanity of all peoples ("We're still talking in
terms of blacks and whites, but we're either all Americans, or
forget it"), had actually had his faith redeemed by a group of
quite disparate working people who hadn't the slightest idea
that elsewhere, internationally elsewhere, this large sad man
was a celebrity.

"I don't know if I could have come out of the
graveyard if it hadn't been for them," Mingus said. "And
then, after a time, Alvin Ailey called. He wanted me to work
with him on what turned out to be 'The Mingus Dances,'
based on my music, that he choreographed for the Joffrey
Ballet. His call, and the care the people in the neighborhood
had been showing, made me start to look at myself. I found I
wasn't so bad after all. So I came out better from having been
down and out."

Mingus talked about a number of ongoing musical projects, interrupting himself to emphasize: "Now that I'm back, I'm going to keep on not being tied down."

I asked him what he meant. It turned out he had been looking over some of his previous albums. "And in the liner notes for one of them," Mingus explained, "a critic had written that I had never pinned myself down so that anyone could say, '*This* is Mingus!'" He just doesn't understand that I don't want to be caught in any one groove. *Everything* I do is Mingus. That's why I don't like to use the word 'jazz' for my work. I write what I think is classical music, too. Of course, there always has to be improvisation in it. A really creative improvisatory solo can be as priceless as Bach or Beethoven. And obviously, if you leave space for improvisers in a symphony—which I intend to do—it's going to be different every time it's performed."

We listened to the tape of another selection from the album Mingus had just recorded. A breeze of woodwinds came through the speakers, but the soft, dancing flow was suddenly fragmented by a slashing alto saxophone followed by an intense, grandly rhapsodic solo on an instrument that at first sounded like a gypsy's oversize guitar but was, of course, Mingus himself *col arco*, bowing the bass.

"Yeah, I got that back, too," Mingus said with pleasure. He nodded his approval of the take, and as the next reel was being opened I noticed on the box that the new album's title was *Let My Children Hear Music*. I asked Mingus what he meant by it.

"A lot of what the kids get to hear," Mingus said, "with rock music being all over the place, is noise. It's so limited in what it expresses, and it's limited in how it expresses what little it does have to say. But kids are able to hear more, much more. Not long ago I played with my band on the Jazzmobile—you know, those free concerts in the streets for kids during the summer. We were in Central Harlem and one of the guys with me said, 'Mingus, you can't play what you usually do for these kids here. They don't dig it.' But I did play what I usually do. And I did more. I took the music as far out as I could and they still liked it.

"All those kids," Mingus was smiling, seeing them again, "following the truck, wanting more. Of course they wanted to hear it. It's *their* music, man. It's their lives. It goes back so far and has so much farther to go."

As I was leaving, Mingus mentioned that he was trying to get Roy Eldridge to do what he called a "walk-on solo" at his forthcoming concert. "I always liked all those older cats," Mingus said. "I always liked to play with them. Nothing ever could keep them down. Look at Roy. Over sixty years old and still growing."

Mingus has a special reason for respecting Eldridge. It goes back to when Mingus was in high school in Los Angeles and Roy Eldridge came through. He was to play with accompaniment by the school band, and in that band was Charles Mingus. "One of the guys in the band, a Negro," Mingus recalls, "was putting down the older players like Roy, saying they couldn't play in tune, couldn't play in a section, and weren't trained at all. This kid was impressed by white musicians. When Roy came I told him some of what this kid had said. Roy looked at me, pointed to his horn, and said very forcefully, 'You see this horn. I play what I feel on it. That's jazz. You'd better find out about the music of your people. Someday you're going to thank me for talking to you like this."

Mingus remembered, and in all the years I have known him he has been pridefully voluble about the blackness of his music. Sometimes, however, he has had to prove just how black it is. There was one night at the Five Spot in New York, when a very black musician standing at the bar was loudly excoriating the less-dark Mingus as the latter was in the middle of a number. "Man," this latter-day herald of Black Consciousness shouted at Mingus, "you're not *black* enough to play the blues."

The man at the bar advanced on Mingus, and the latter started to lay down his bass, preparatory to continuing the dialogue with fists. But Mingus changed his mind, picked up the bass, and roared into a bass solo which plunged so deeply into the blues that his tormentor was quite literally taken aback. (It was as if Mingus's bass had turned into a cross before an oncoming Dracula.)

On the other hand, although Mingus is acutely conscious of racism in its multifarious manifestations, he has also felt it imperative to think beyond race. "It's not only a question of color any more," he told me some years ago. "It's getting deeper than that. I mean it's getting more and more difficult for a man or woman to just love. People are getting so fragmented, and part of that is that fewer and fewer people are making a real effort any more to find exactly who they are and to build on that knowledge. Most people are forced to do things they don't want to most of the time, and so they get to the point where they feel they no longer have any choice about anything important, including who they are. We create our own slavery. But I'm going to keep on getting through and finding out the kind of man I am through my music. That's the one place I can be free."

This concept of jazz as an essential route to self-liberation and self-identification is common to the history of the music.

When I was a boy, growing up on jazz, I wasn't conscious of it as freedom music in this sense, but I was aware of what seemed to me an extraordinary vitality in these jazz musicians. Not always off the stand, but invariably on the stand. Each had so singular a sound and way of phrasing, each was so free and sometimes so daring in his self-expression. Much more so than the classical musicians I also heard as a boy. Much more so than any other adults I knew. To me these jazz musicians were heroic as they played, heroically individualistic—and free.

As I got to know more of them, I began to see jazz musicians in a somewhat less luminous light. They were fallible and some could be obnoxious and even harmful to themselves and to others, but I was still struck at how much life there was in them. Mingus is right. Most people do create their own slavery, do spend their working time at being smaller than they could be. For the jazz musician, however, the music, as John Coltrane once said, is "the whole question of life itself." And as a number of jazzmen have also emphasized, what you live and how you live becomes an instant, integral part of what you play each night, so that jazz is a continual autobiography, or rather a continuum of intersecting autobiographies, one's own and those of the musicians with whom one plays.

The jazz musician, then, is judged not only by his musicianship and conception, but also by the quality of his emotional life as it is formed in and through his music. This has nothing to do with how "noble" or "base" those emotions are, let alone with how "moral" or "immoral" the musician's life is. It has to do with how open and how deeply plumbed those emotions are and then, of course, with how well they are transmuted into art by musicianship and musical conception.

I have known jazz musicians I would characterize as evil—by the way they treated others—who were, however, utterly absorbing in their performances because they did play who they were, without euphemism, and so their music was true, however malignantly true. Again I have to emphasize that they were also first-class musicians, otherwise their personal revelations would have been of no musical moment. The point is that of all sophisticated forms of music, jazz is the most self-revealing, the music where there is the least room for the performer to hide who he or she is.

Some musicians obviously are more continually arresting than others because they are more complicated emotionally—and thereby, in jazz, they have to become more complicated artistically to express their abundance of ambivalences. John Coltrane, for instance, was perpetually examining and reexamining his life; and since there was no division between his music and his life, the recordings he has left—and the memories of his "live" performances—are a fascinating odyssey of perhaps the most philosophical (in music, not in words) of all jazz musicians so far.

Charles Mingus also is continually exploring and assessing himself. "I'm trying," he says, "to play the truth of what I am. The reason it's difficult is because I'm changing all the time."

And so he is, including outside change. I have seen Mingus huge, Mingus shrunken in shape, Mingus in between, Mingus jocular, Mingus hopelessly brooding, Mingus surprised into elation by a sideman's solo, Mingus as the loneliest man in the world. And Mingus achieving in his music what he said of Charlie Parker: "Bird sometimes could make the whole room feel as he did."

Of all the musicians in jazz, Mingus can be the most unpredictable and uncategorizable. Or, as he says at the beginning of *Beneath the Underdog:* "In other words, I am three. One man stands forever in the middle unconcerned, unmoved, watching, waiting to be allowed to express what he sees to the other two. The second man is like a frightened animal that attacks for fear of being attacked. Then there's an over-loving gentle person who lets people into the uttermost sacred temple of his being and he'll take insults and be trusting and sign contracts without reading them and get talked down to working cheap or for nothing, and when he realizes what's been done to him he feels like killing and destroying everything around him including himself for being so stupid. But he can't—he goes back inside himself."

Where he finds more than three. Many more than three.

Musically, these many Minguses have, through the years, created and sustained a number of the more memorable small combos in jazz history. Perhaps because he himself is subject to so many nuances of mood, Mingus has been responsive to an unusually wide diversity of temperaments among the musicians he has employed. And he has shaped these musicians in ways that result not only in an unmistakable *Mingus* collective sound, but also in the markedly enhanced individual growth of the musicians under his sometimes imperious command.

As Whitney Balliett once explained the first part of the process: "Mingus . . . asks of his musicians even more than the classical composer asks of his—that they carry both the letter and the spirit of his basic composition over into their own improvisations instead of using them as a trigger for their own ruminations."

The second part of the Mingus process—the practically forced growth of the musicians, individually—has been attested to by nearly all the Mingus alumni with whom I've discussed the subject. They are not uncritical alumni (in the Mingus academy the clashing of personalities sounds the hours), but they agree that they left the Mingus workshop knowing more about themselves, musically and personally, than when they came. Mingus would not allow musicians to just assume roles in his microcosm. He has craved reality—of feeling, of intellect, of technique. As much reality of his own life and emotions as each player could put into the music. And Mingus has kept insisting, at each stage, that more reality was possible than each player had so far shown the energy to reveal.

"You had to keep stretching yourself while you were with Mingus," an ex-sideman told me. "He just wouldn't let you coast. Even in public—you've seen it—he'd yell at you in the middle of a solo to stop playing just licks and get into yourself. Christ, he had more confidence in what we were capable of than we had."

At his best, Mingus with a small combo has sometimes reached the level of highly creative fusion that Duke Ellington achieved with an orchestra. He has created a microcosm entirely his own—the citizens of which, however, learn more about themselves the more they learn how most probingly to play Mingus's own music.

An illuminating sketch of Mingus the combiner-expander is that of Alan Weitz in the *Village Voice* in the fall of 1971. He was writing of Mingus during a jammed night at the Village Vanguard in New York: "There was Mingus, sitting on a stool, the body of the bass leaning against his stomach, shouting, conducting, singing, and playing a line that often lent the group support and held it together and at other times intricately wove in and out of the other instruments."

Among the sources of Mingus's music is the spiralingly emotional collective music-making of the church. "A lot of my music," he says, "comes from church. All the music I heard when I was a very young child was church music. I was eight or nine years old before I heard an Ellington record on the radio. My father went to the Methodist church; my stepmother would take me to the Holiness church, which was too raw for my father. He didn't dig my mother going there. At the Holiness church the congregation gives their testimonial before the Lord, they confess their sins and sing and shout and do a little Holy Rolling. Some preachers cast out demons; they call their dialogue 'talking in tongues' or talking in an unknown tongue (language that the Devil can't understand). People went into trances and the congregation's response was wilder and more uninhibited than in the Methodist church. The blues was in the Holiness churches—moaning, riffs and that sort of thing between the audience and the preacher."

Mingus heard this church music in the Watts section of Los Angeles, where he was brought a few months after he was born in Nogales, Arizona, on April 22, 1922. His first instrument was a trombone. Then came the cello and eventually the bass. For five years he studied the bass with H. Rheinschagen, a former member of the New York Philharmonic.

Mingus has described his evolution into and through technique to that fusion of instrument and player that is essential to the highest order of jazz improvising: "I'd practice the hardest things incessantly. The third finger is seldom used, so I used it all the time. What happened, however, is that for a while I concentrated on speed and technique almost as ends in themselves. I aimed at scaring all the other bass players. I stood right, and I was conscious of every note I ran. There seemed to be no problems I couldn't solve. Then one night, when I was eighteen or nineteen, all this changed. . . . I began playing and didn't stop for a long time. It was suddenly *me;* it wasn't the bass any more. Now I'm not conscious of the instrument as an instrument when I play. And I don't dig any longer thinking in terms of whether one man is a 'better' bassist than another. You're up there—everyone is—trying to express yourself. It's like a preacher, in a sense. And the instrument, any instrument, shouldn't get in the way."

A key influence on the rapidly growing musician was Duke Ellington. ("When I first heard Duke Ellington in person I almost jumped out of the balcony. One piece excited me so much that I screamed.") Mingus also listened to classical music—particularly Debussy, Ravel, and Richard Strauss—and began composing. Like Cecil Taylor, when the latter was in the early stages of his career, Mingus didn't particularly care if he was criticized for revealing "European" influences in his work because he was as certain of the eventual wholeness of his compositional identity as he was of his already formed instrumental identity. Besides, then as now he scorned narrowing musical categories. He prefers, for instance, not to have his music categorized as "jazz." It is Mingus music.

After working around Los Angeles, Mingus played with Louis Armstrong, Kid Ory, Lionel Hampton, Red Norvo, Billy Taylor, Charlie Parker, Duke Ellington, Bud Powell, and Art Tatum among others—a rather full spectrum of jazz seasoning. Being considered sufficiently skillful to meet the challenge of playing with Art Tatum was a particular delight for Mingus, because years before, in Los Angeles, when he had once tried to sit in with Tatum that magisterial pianist had laughed at him.

For nearly twenty-five years Mingus has been on his own, heading his own groups, continually searching into himself and into the society around him for ways to battle those forces which diminish our lives when there is so little time to live those lives to their capacities. He has been down and out and up again but he has never, to use his term, been "placid." That word came up when Mingus was describing what he called the beboppers during the early years of modern jazz. "At times," Mingus said, "they seemed to me to have been too placid."

"What do you mean 'placid?'"

"Well," Mingus said, "the beboppers were the groupies of that time. Charlie Parker was not a bebopper, but those who copied him were. And a bunch of people who copy somebody and all sound alike—they're placid."

Mingus, down or up, has also continued to adhere to the jazz credo, his credo, of not being swayed from doing what he hears and feels—no matter what conventional authority dictates as being hip at any given time. Mingus tells the story of how, as a young man, he greatly enjoyed playing in the New Orleans-rooted band of the venerable Kid Ory. "But while I was in that band," Mingus says, "Fats Navarro was telling me, 'That's not it, Mingus; that's what they *used* to do.' Well, I'm not going to worry about that sort of thing any more, I said to myself at the time. I'm going to be *me*. And nowadays, if Bird himself were to come back to life, I wouldn't do something just because he did it. I'd have to feel it, too."

jazz is:

Cootie Williams, the loner and sharp listener of the Duke Ellington band, saying of Charlie Parker in the early 1940's: "Louis Armstrong changed all the brass players around, but after Bird, *all* of the instruments had to change—drums, piano, bass, trombones, trumpets, saxophones, everything."

Birdland in the early 1950's. A wealthy, rather arrogant young woman is writing an article about Charlie Parker for a national magazine. As **Miles Davis** gets off the stand, she stops him, tells him her assignment, and asks, "Why did they call him Bird?"

Miles looks at her for a long time, while deciding whether or not to answer, and finally says, "Because he squeaked on his horn."

"That's not true," the young woman says acidly. "I know why. I found it out. But I won't tell you."

Miles grimaces. "So you got a secret now. I'll tell you another. Bird was a friend of mine. I used to put him to bed sometimes with the needle still in his arm and him bleeding all over the place. He used to pawn my suitcase and take all my money. You going to put that in your article?"

Dizzy Gillespie in the summer of 1975, about to

leave for the Montreux Jazz Festival after having triumphed at the Newport Jazz Festival in New York. The most successful survivor of the initial creators of modern jazz, Dizzy is asked about Bird, and says: "He wasn't strong enough to last long. It's hard out there for a black man in this society. If you let all those pressures get to you and then start to slide all the way along with them, they will do you in."

The second of Norman Granz's Jazz at the Philharmonic concerts, January 29, 1946, with Lester Young, Willie Smith, Charlie Ventura, Al Killian, and Charlie Parker, among others. Says pianist **John Lewis** of Parker's music that night: "Bird made a blues out of *Lady Be Good*. That solo made old men out of everyone on stage that night."

Ralph Ellison, getting to the core of Bird in *Shadow and Act:* "In attempting to escape the role, at once sub- and super-human, in which he found himself, he sought to outrage his public into an awareness of his most human pain. Instead, he made himself notorious and in the end became unsure whether his fans came to enjoy his art or to be entertained by the 'world's greatest junky,' the 'supreme hipster.'"

the great speckled bird

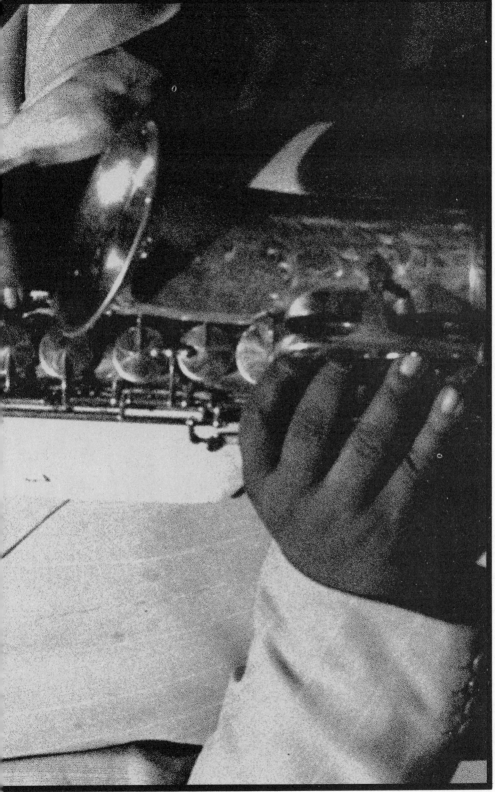

Charlie Parker

Ben Webster

There have been a number of instances in jazz history of the incandescent hero-as-world-overturning-improviser eventually plunging, like Icarus, into burnt-out extinction. Bix Beiderbecke, Bunny Berigan, Fats Navarro, and, way back, Buddy Bolden were some of these charred legends. But there has been—so far—no more daring, dangerous, revolutionary flight than that of Charlie Parker. And no terminal descent that has been more assiduously mythologized than that of Charlie Parker. He is the paradigm of the jazzman-as-victim, though some would say he was more the victim of himself than of society. To which Dizzy Gillespie would answer, "Where do you draw the line between the two if you're a black man?"

Charlie Parker was born in Kansas City, Kansas, on August 29, 1920, his father a small-time singer and dancer, and later a Pullman chef. Some seven or eight years later the family moved across the river to Olive Street, near the nightlife center of Kansas City, Missouri. Charlie Parker's father left home before the boy had finished grammar school and he grew up loved, indulged, and not a little spoiled by his mother, Addie.

Parker, though desultorily interested in music as a young boy, didn't become passionately intrigued with horn play until he was in high school. After an unsatisfying experience with the cumbersome baritone horn, Charlie switched to an alto saxophone which his mother had bought him. He became the fourth member of the reed section of an amateur dance band, the Deans of Swing, in his high school. Parker was barely fourteen, and as bassist Gene Ramey recalls, "Bird wasn't doing anything, musically speaking, at that period. In fact, he was the saddest thing in the band, and the other members gave him something of a hard time."

Bird quit school around 1935 to become a full-time musician or rather, at first, an earnest, vulnerable apprentice.

The story of his apprenticeship is worth detailing, for it reveals that even Bird had to look hard and long to find himself musically.

The musical scene in Kansas City at the time Bird first became an actively listening part of it was described some years later in *Down Beat:* ". . . the joints were running full blast from 9 p.m. to 5 a.m. Usual pay was $1.25 a night. ...There were about 15 bands in town, with Pete Johnson's crew at the Sunset Café one of the most popular. Harlan Leonard was in town then, along with George Lee's and Bus Moten's little bands. Lester Young, Herschel Evans, and Eddie Barefield were playing around. Top local pianists were Roselle Claxton, Mary Lou Williams, Edith Williams, and Basie."

Jo Jones, also in Kansas City during this period, adds that there was also a player named Walter Knight. "I have never heard anybody play a sax like he did in my life. I can hear a little of it in Charlie Parker," Jones recalled.

But it's likely that another man active in Kansas City at that time was the direct influence on Bird, if anyone ever was. Again it's Jo Jones who recalls the context: "The greatest band I ever heard in my life was Walter Page's Blue Devils band. . . . In the band was Buster Smith. Buster was an alto player who used to be called Prof, and he was Charlie Parker's musical father." Ben Webster and Jimmy Rushing, also on the scene at the time, agreed with Jo.

Charlie Parker himself admitted his interest in Smith along with others. As Leonard Feather wrote in *Inside Be-Bop:* "Charlie's evolution as a modern jazzman cannot be ascribed to any one influence. During his first years around jazz, he listened to Herschel Evans and Lester Young, both with Basie; to the late Chu Berry, and to Andy Kirk's tenor man, the late Dick Wilson. He admired Johnny Hodges, Willie

Smith and Benny Carter, and especially an alto player named Buster Smith, who did most of the arranging for Count Basie's original band in Kansas City. 'I used to quit every job to go with Buster,' says Charlie."

At another time in his life Parker pointed out to an interviewer that although he admired the musicians just listed, almost all played with a pronounced vibrato. He himself disliked vibrato, as evidenced by his own approach. Lester Young used less vibrato than anyone and Bird recalled, "I was crazy about Lester. He played so clean and beautiful. But I wasn't influenced by Lester. Our ideas ran on differently."

Actually, it does appear that a large percentage of what Charlie became musically he developed by himself—the hard way. "One time, when I was in my teens, jamming in a Kansas City club, I was doing all right until I tried doing double tempo on *Body and Soul*," Charlie remembered. "Everybody fell out laughing. I went home and cried and didn't want to play again for three months."

Gene Ramey remembers meeting a downcast Bird on the street. (As an index of the musical liveliness of Kansas City around this time, Count Basie was playing on one side of that street and Duke Ellington on the other, with the local musicians running from one club to the other during intermissions.) Bird told Ramey that while there were an awful lot of jam sessions in town, he, Bird, was one of the few musicians who were never allowed to sit in.

The ban relaxed, however, and one night Ramey and Bird sat in at the Reno Club where Count Basie was working. Jo Jones was on drums, and Bird, though starting well, suddenly fell out of the key, couldn't find it again, and then lost the time. Jo Jones stopped drumming. In the awful silence Jones took one of his cymbals and threw it at Parker's feet (as he was to do many years later in New York when Cecil Taylor tried to sit in with a group that included the fiercely exacting drummer). There was laughter, and Bird, humiliated, packed up his horn and left the club.

"I'll fix these cats," Bird told Ramey. "Everybody laughing at me now, but just you wait and see."

Bird proceeded to woodshed, memorizing Lester Young solos from recordings and, during a job in the Ozarks, acquiring postgraduate chordal knowledge from guitarist Efferge Ware. "It was from Ware," Ramey is convinced, "that Bird fully learned the relationship of the chords and how to weave melodies into them."

When Bird came back to Kansas City from the Ozarks he had so grown musically that he began to get plenty of work and had no more problems holding his own in jam sessions. "Bird," says Ramey, "had his own sound by that time. Clean and without much vibrato. He hadn't given up on his strange ideas, stuff like double-timing and weird modulations in and out of key, but they made a little sense now. . . . He sounded almost exactly like Lester Young, Lester playing alto, but with something else of his own that was beginning to come through. The difference [between Bird before he left for the mountains and after] was unbelievable."

In time, however, jobs became scarce in Kansas City; there were tensions at home with Rebecca, his first wife; and Bird, pawning his horn, left town for a period of scruffy wandering.

He showed up in Chicago at a session at which Billy Eckstine was in attendance and years afterward described: "The vogue before the war was to have a breakfast dance on one day of the week. Every club in Chicago, at some time or another, would have a breakfast dance, with the show going on at six thirty in the morning.

"One spot there, the 65 Club, had a breakfast dance

one morning, and they had a little combo with King Kolax on trumpet; a kid named Goon Gardner, who could swing like mad, on alto; John Simmons on bass; and Kansas Fields, drums.

"It was more or less a jam show, for after the show all the musicians would blow in there. We were standing around one morning when a guy comes up that looks like he just got off a freight car, the raggedest guy you'd want to see at this moment. And he asks Goon, 'Say, man, can I come up and blow your horn?'

"Now Goon was always a kind of lazy cat. Anybody that wanted to get on the stand and blow, just as long as Goon could go to the bar and talk with the chicks, it was all right with him. So he said, 'Yes, man, go ahead.'

"And this cat gets up there, and I'm telling you he blew the bell off that thing! It was Charlie Parker, just come in from Kansas City on a freight train. I guess Bird was no more than about eighteen then, but playing like you never heard—wailing alto then. . . .

"He blew so much until he upset everybody in the joint, and Goon took him home, gave him some clothes to put on, and got him a few gigs. Bird didn't have a horn, naturally, so Goon lent him a clarinet to go and make gigs on. According to what Goon told me, one day he looked for Bird, and Bird, the clarinet, and all was gone—back somewhere."

The somewheres was New York and Bird himself took up the story at this point in an interview some twelve years later in *Down Beat:* "For three months he washed dishes in Jimmy's Chicken Shack in Harlem. This was at the time Art Tatum was spellbinding late-hour Shack habitues. Charlie got $9 a week and meals. Then [when Tatum left] he quit and bummed around a while, sleeping where he could.

"'I didn't have any troubles with cops,' he recalls. 'I

was lucky. I guess it was because I looked so young.' There was a series of skimpy jobs, such as a gig at Monroe's Uptown House where Charlie sometimes got 40 or 50 cents a night. If business was good, he might get up to $6.

"'Nobody paid me much mind then except Bobby Moore, one of Count Basie's trumpet players,' Charlie said. 'He liked me. Everybody else was trying to get me to sound like Benny Carter.'"

During this same period Bird experienced an epiphany, or so he said later. At a chili house on Seventh Avenue in Harlem Bird used to jam with a guitarist named Buddy Fleet. He had become bored with the standard chord changes, even the advanced standard chord changes, and, he later told an interviewer, "I kept thinking there's bound to be something else. I could hear it sometimes, but I couldn't play it." Then one night, as he and Fleet were improvising on *Cherokee*, Bird discovered that by making a melody line of the higher intervals of a chord—and then using appropriate changes for that new chord-derived melody line—he could indeed play what he had been hearing.

Bird went back to Kansas City for his father's funeral, played with Harland Leonard's band for five weeks (being asked to leave for chronic lateness), and joined Jay McShann's band, coming out of Kansas City.

Gene Ramey has described the McShann band of that period and the restless Parker: "The Jay McShann band was the only one I've ever known that seemed to spend all its spare time jamming or rehearsing. We used to jam on trains and buses, and as soon as we got into a town, we'd try to find somebody's house where we could hold a session. All this was inspired by Bird because the new ideas he was bringing to the band made everybody anxious to play.

"We were at a club in New Orleans on one occasion,

playing a one-nighter, when we were informed by Decca that we were due for a record session in a couple of weeks. McShann suggested that we get together and do something real quick. It was one of those real warm days in New Orleans, but we got together and had a little session and the ideas came across. I guess in about forty-five minutes we had *The Jumpin' Blues* ready. This arrangement was all a 'head' put together by Bird, and the record featured one of his first great solos on wax.

"Bird was one of the reasons it was such a happy-go-lucky band. He used to say: 'If you come on a band tense, you're going to play tense. If you come a little bit foolish, act just a little bit foolish, and let yourself go, better ideas will come.'

"Everything had a musical significance for Bird. He got into his music all the sounds right around him—the swish of a car speeding down a highway, the hum of the wind as it goes through the leaves. Everything had a musical message for him. If he heard a dog bark, he would say the dog was speaking. . . . And maybe some girl would walk past on the dance floor while he was playing, and something she might do, or an expression on her face, would give him an idea for something to play on his solo. As soon as he would do that, we were all so close we'd all understand just what he meant. He might be looking another way, but as soon as he played that little phrase, everybody would look up and get the message. . . .

"Now that I look back on it, Bird was so far ahead of his time that nobody really appreciated just how radical his ideas were. For instance, we used to jam *Cherokee* a lot, and Bird had a way of starting on a B natural against the B flat chord and he would run a cycle against that—and probably it would only be two or three bars before we got to the channel [middle part] that he would come back to the basic changes.

"In those days we used to call it 'running out of key.' Bird used to sit and try to explain to us what he was doing. I am sure that at that time nobody else in the band could even play, for example, the channel to *Cherokee*. So Bird used to play a series of *Tea for Two* phrases against that channel, and since this was a melody that could easily be remembered it gave the other guys something to play during those bars."

After traveling to Texas and then the Carolinas, back to Chicago and Kansas City, the McShann band headed to New York and the Savoy. In New York Bird quickly attracted musicians' attention, both with the McShann band and at Monroe's in Harlem, where he doubled at night.

Kenny Clarke, a drummer who had already been developing rhythmic changes that were to be central to modern jazz, recalls: "We went to listen to Bird at Monroe's for no other reason than the fact that he sounded like Prez, like Lester Young. That is, until we found out that he had something of his own to offer. He was into figures I thought I had invented for drums. Bird was twice as fast as Prez and into harmony Prez hadn't touched. Bird was running the same way that I, and musicians who thought as I did, were going. I mean people like Dizzy and Monk. But Bird was way out ahead of us. He was playing things rhythmically and harmonically we'd never heard before."

In Ross Russell's biography of Charlie Parker, *Bird Lives!*, Clarke adds that he and his musical colleagues persuaded Parker to move from Monroe's to Minton's. "Pretty soon Minton's got to be a bad place for older cats. Dizzy began coming up regularly and that gave us the four key instruments—trumpet, alto, piano [Thelonious Monk], and drums. That, plus a good bass, was the band of the future. One night, after weeks of trying, Dizzy cut Roy Eldridge. It was one night out of many that he'd been trying, but it meant a great deal. Roy had been top dog for years. We closed our ranks after that."

Parker left the Jay McShann band at the end of 1941, worked intermittently and unsatisfyingly with other bands, and finally joined an Earl Hines orchestra which included Dizzy Gillespie, Benny Harris, and Sarah Vaughan. Hines needed a tenor saxophonist at the time, and so he bought a tenor for Bird. With the band rehearsing days, Parker and other sidemen jammed at Minton's by night.

Billy Eckstine, then singing with the Hines band, recalls the night Ben Webster, the huge-toned, deeply swinging tenor with Duke Ellington, walked into the club: "Charlie's up on the stand and he's wailing the tenor. Ben had never heard Bird, you know, and he says, 'What the hell is that up there? Man, is that cat crazy?' And he goes up and snatches the horn out of Bird's hands, saying, 'That horn ain't *supposed* to sound that fast.'

"But that night," Eckstine continues, "Ben walked all over town telling everyone, 'Man, I heard a guy—I swear he's going to make everybody crazy on tenor.' The fact is Bird never felt tenor, never liked it. But he was playing like mad on the damn thing."

As with Jay McShann, Bird was not a model of professional responsibility while with Earl Hines. Months before Hines had actually hired Bird, he had called McShann to tell him he wanted his alto player but didn't want to poach. McShann, however, had told Hines: "The sooner you take him, the better. He just passed out in front of the microphone right in the middle of *Cherokee*."

So Hines had been forewarned. This incident with McShann—and others to be related which took place while Bird was with Hines—indicate, moreover, that the notion in later years that "society," "the system," eventually caused the terminal disintegration of Bird has to be measured in the context of what Bird did to himself for much of his life. The other members of the McShann and Hines bands had, after all, also been black and had also been certainly sensitive to the overwhelming racism in the society at large. But it was Bird who chronically goofed off.

"Bird," Billy Eckstine has written in the *Melody Maker*, "used to miss as many shows as he would make [with Hines]. Half the time we couldn't find Bird; he'd be sitting up somewhere sleeping. So he often missed the first shows, and Earl used to fine him blind. . . . We got on him too because we were more or less a clique. We told him, 'When you don't show, man, it's a drag because the band don't sound right. You know, four reeds up there and everything written for five.' We kind of shamed him.

"So one time we were working the Paradise Theatre in Detroit, and Bird says, 'I ain't gonna miss no more. I'm going to stay in the theatre all night to make sure I'm here.'

"We answered, 'Okay. That's your business. Just make the show, huh?'

"Sure enough, we come to work the next morning, we get on the stand—no Bird. As usual. We think, so, he said he was going to make the show and he didn't make it.

"This is the gospel truth. After we played the whole show, the curtains closed, and we're coming off the band cart, when all of a sudden we hear a noise. We look under the stand, and here comes Bird out from underneath. He had been under there asleep through the entire show!

"Another thing happened at the Paradise. You see, Bird often used to take his shoes off while he was up on the stand and put his feet on top of his shoes.

"He wore those dark glasses all the time he was playing, and sometimes, while the acts were on, he would nod and go off to sleep. This particular time, the act was over and it was a band specialty now. So Bird was sitting there with his horn still in his mouth, doing the best faking in the world for Earl's benefit.

"Earl used to swear he was awake. Bird was the only man I knew who could sleep with his jaws poked out to look like he was playing, see? So this day he sat up there, sound asleep, and it came time for his solo.

"Scoops Carey, who sat next to him in the reed section, nudged him and said, 'Hey, Bird, wake up, you're on.' And Bird ran right out to the mike in his stocking feet; just jumped up and forgot his shoes and ran out front and started wailing."

Bird was with Hines for ten months, playing tenor. He was making $105 a week, the largest sum he'd ever earned. (He used to average $55 to $60 with McShann). But the salaries started going down as the band hit an Army-camp tour in a package involved with a beer company. There were also booking hassles, and finally Charlie dropped out in Washington in late 1943.

Unfortunately, the Hines band that possessed all this explosive talent capped by Dizzy and Bird never got a chance to record. The recording ban had gone into effect August 1, 1942, and lasted all the time Bird was in the band and beyond, into November, 1944.

After Bird worked for a time with Sir Charles Thompson, there came other gigs, including stays with Cootie Williams, Andy Kirk, and Carroll Dickerson in Chicago. In 1944 Bird went on the road with a Billy Eckstine band which included Dizzy Gillespie, Sarah Vaughan, Gene Ammons, and Art Blakey.

The Eckstine band, however, was too experimental to make it commercially at that time and finally evaporated.

Bird, meanwhile, had tired of the big-band scene and returned to New York for the freedom of small combos. His influence grew more and more rapidly as he played frequently along 52nd Street in bands led by Ben Webster, Dizzy Gillespie, and a group Bird himself headed at the Three Deuces with Miles Davis, then eighteen, on trumpet. He also made records through 1944–45, starting with his first small band date under Tiny Grimes on Savoy, followed by sessions with Clyde Hart, Dizzy Gillespie, Sarah Vaughan, Red Norvo, Slim Gaillard, and dates under his own name on Savoy that included *Ko-Ko*, *Billie's Bounce*, *Now's the Time*, and *Thriving from a Riff* (which contained a chorus that later became *Anthropology*).

Bird's renown among musicians in the East accelerated and his records expanded the impact across the country and eventually into Europe. Tony Scott, then a youngster fresh from Juilliard and an Army stint, describes Bird's impact on a characteristic newcomer to jazz: "The first time The Street heard Bird, I think, was around 1942. Bird came in one night and sat in with Don Byas. He blew *Cherokee* and everybody just flipped.

"Then, when Bird and Diz hit The Street regularly a couple of years later, everybody was astounded once again and nobody could get near their way of playing music. Finally, however, Bird and Diz made records; and at that point guys could imitate it and go from there."

In late 1945 Bird went out to the West Coast and a date at Billy Berg's with a band led by Dizzy Gillespie that included Milt Jackson, Ray Brown, Al Haig, and Stan Levey. Bird now was close to the breaking point both physically and emotionally.

The time-bomb of Bird's collapse had been set many years before. Bird was to describe the process that brought him to the chasm in California in a *Metronome* interview with

Leonard Feather two years after the event: "Charlie was around show people when he was very young. 'It all came from being introduced too early to night life,' he told Feather. 'When you're not mature enough to know what's happening—well, you goof.'"

Parker had started his heroin habit at the age of fifteen. It remained with him for most of the rest of his life. Like most addicts he became a reasonably expert hustler—"borrowing" money, clothes, and sometimes horns.

All his appetites were large. As prodigious, for instance, as was Parker's capacity for drugs, so it also was for sex. He lived hard; and a hedonist would say he lived most fully. But between swift peaks of pleasure there was constant scuffling. Or, as he told Leonard Feather, "I became bitter, hard, cold. I was always on a panic—couldn't buy clothes or a good place to live."

The breakdown, the first widely visible breakdown, took place during that mid-forties engagement on the West Coast where, as Parker felt, "Nobody understood our kind of music. They *hated* it." Yet Dizzy Gillespie, experiencing the same hostility, did not collapse. But Dizzy had not already weakened himself by years of addiction and other ways of self-destruction.

At Billy Berg's Bird missed sets and even whole nights. Lucky Thompson was hired as a kind of permanent substitute and he was often needed. Dizzy left for the East and Bird remained—harried, rushing closer to disintegration.

He continued making records, recording now for Dial, a label owned by Ross Russell. With Miles Davis, Lucky, Dodo Marmorosa, and others he cut *A Night in Tunisia*, *Yardbird Suite*, *Ornithology*, *and Moose the Mooche*, among other performances that have become quasi-legendary. But Bird had been hanging onto a thread all this time and it finally broke. "As his craving for and dependence on dope grew worse," Feather later described Bird's descent, "he developed violent tics. On the night of July 29, 1946, his limbs and muscles jerking and twitching uncontrollably, he went to a recording studio on a session organized by Ross Russell. . . . He was only able to struggle through two sides before he left. (A fictionalized account of that date is Elliott Grennard's "Sparrow's Last Jump," *Harper's*, May, 1947.)

"That night he set fire to his hotel room and ran down into the lobby naked and screaming. Russell helped with the arrangements in sending him to Carmarillo State Hospital after his arrest, but to his dying day Parker never forgave Russell for releasing *Lover Man*, recorded on that disastrous night and a shamefully unrepresentative sample of his work."

Parker was at Camarillo for almost seven months. When he was released he recorded again for Dial in February, 1947. He sounded recovered, and was playing brilliantly again.

Back in New York in 1947, Bird headed a series of small combos, continued to record, toured with Jazz at the Philharmonic in 1948, was in Europe in the summer of 1949, worked the new Birdland club (named in his notorious honor) in 1950, when he also signed a new recording contract, this one with Norman Granz, that offered him more security than any recording agreement he had yet had. By this point Bird was also getting broader recognition from the jazz audience— though not from the general public. Starting in 1950, he won the *Down Beat* poll every year, as well as almost all other ballotings in both American and foreign jazz publications.

For a time Parker recorded and toured with strings, the touring being much less orderly than the recordings. Never the most stable of performers, before or after Camarillo, Bird became increasingly unpredictable, as Ross Russell details in his biography of Parker. Trying to avoid narcotics he became a sometimes heavy drinker, the latter addiction leading to a serious ulcer attack which hospitalized him. Still, there were occasional periods of surface calm and highly expert playing. But more and more frequently Bird acted bizarrely. And when not bizarre he was often desolate.

One night, going down the stairs to Birdland, I saw Bird, tears streaming down his face, coming up. He stopped and said, "I've got to see you. It's very important. *Very*. I'll call you tomorrow." He never did.

In March, 1954, Parker's three-year-old daughter, Pree, died suddenly of pneumonia while he was on the road and that grief never left him. Meanwhile, his behavior grew more strange. In the fall of that year, during an engagement at Birdland with a string group, Parker started lacerating his sidemen on stand and then summarily fired them. Having been drinking all that evening, he topped his straw-boss performance by slumping into a chair on the bandstand and falling asleep. Later that night he attempted suicide.

Shocked by how close he had come to actually ending himself, Bird stopped drinking and agreed to report regularly to the out-patient clinic at Bellevue for psychotherapy. The cracked center would not hold, however. His drinking began again, and Bird was now traveling from city to city as a single, working with local rhythm sections. There were times when he still played well, but much of his work was considerably below what listeners expected of him. "He's just an historical figure now," one musician said sadly.

On March 4, 1955, Parker figured in an utterly dismaying scene, the most painful I have ever witnessed in more than thirty years of jazz listening. He had been booked for two nights at Birdland with Bud Powell, Charles Mingus, Kenny Dorham, and Art Blakey. Powell, mentally awry and drunk besides, began the evening by insulting Bird ("You ain't play-ing shit no more") and then being himself unable to play with even minimal coherence. After Parker and Powell exchanged bitter curses on stand, Powell smashed the keyboard and walked off. Then for what seemed to be an awfully long, oppressive time, Bird just stood at the mike calling again and again, "Bud Powell! Bud Powell!"

A disappearing soul calling out to a spirit already irredeemably hidden from everyone, including itself.

The other musicians tried rather bravely, and poig-nantly, to make some kind of musical sense out of the void until Charles Mingus came to the mike and said, "Ladies and gentlemen, please don't associate me with any of this. This is not jazz. These are sick people."

Finally the stage was empty.

Wednesday of the next week, in the apartment of a friend, Baroness Pannonica de Koenigswarter, a woman who was also a genuine friend of Thelonious Monk, Art Blakey, and other jazz musicians, Bird died. Among the causes of death were stomach ulcers, pneumonia, advanced cirrhosis of the liver, and a possible heart attack. The attending physician, basing his judgment on the physical condition of the corpse, estimated Bird's age as between fifty and sixty. He was thirty-four.

The Sunday afternoon before he died, Bird was to have played at the Open Door. The Open Door was a large, perpetually barren-feeling room (even when filled) in a drab, past-caring-to-care section of Greenwich Village. He had played there several times before at Sunday sessions. This Sunday he played not at all. He made an appearance, but all the time he was there he ignored his horn. At one point a friend, another musician, found him in the men's room. Bird was looking at himself in the washroom mirror. He was slowly, carefully and firmly putting himself down in a conversation with the face in the mirror. The conversation went on for some time, adding the newcomer in an odd trialogue. Finally Bird looked hard at the mirror and harshly called the image the worst enemy he had. But, the other musician observed drily, "you'll never have a friend closer to you than that." Bird laughed and went out into the club. But he didn't play.

This same musician tells how Bird would often clam up for several hours, not say a word to anyone. Then, in the same evening, he might suddenly talk for a long stretch—and talk with brilliance.

"God knows," this musician said after Bird's death, "we all owed him so much, all of us who played modern. But which of us could afford him? He'd come to my place and stay for a time, and I'd share whatever I had with him. But eventually, if I wasn't getting many gigs, I'd run out of resources myself and he'd go somewhere else. Who could afford him? I mean that literally. And I mean it the other way, too. Which of us could pay him what we owed him?"

"You know," this musician said as an afterthought, "in one thing he was consistent. He was wonderful with children." Chan Parker, with whom he lived last, has a young daughter from a previous marriage, a child of unusual sensitivity. The child needed love, very much love. Bird gave it to her without reservation.

"Bird," says Chan, "was a gentle man although he hid it much of the time." Chan tells of Bird's delight in shopping in joke shops for such child-surprising excitements as a can labeled peanut brittle which exploded on opening into a swirling of snakes. When he came home from the road, whether he had much money or barely any, he'd bring presents for the kids.

Bird was ambivalent about the road. "There were sections of the country he didn't want to work," Chan recalls. "The West Coast because of the bad memories of what happened there. And the South for obvious reasons. He went South with the Stan Kenton tour the year before he died because so much loot was involved. But ordinarily he didn't want to work west of Chicago or south of Washington. He didn't like all the places he worked within those boundaries either. 'Why,' he said once, 'am I playing in cellars?' And he was bruised again each time the police shook him down in a new town. And some of the club owners were far from human to him.

"He was always hoping to study, maybe with composers like Edgar Varèse or Stefan Wolpe. He knew them both, was friendly with Varèse, and had met Wolpe through Tony Scott, who had studied with him. It's kind of ironic. The guys in the Metropolitan Opera orchestra called and sent condolences when he died."

As far back as 1949 Bird was talking about how he wanted to study more, though he never did. John Wilson and Mike Levin reported in an illuminating *Down Beat* interview of that year: "For the future, he'd like to go to the Academy of Music in Paris for a couple of years, then relax for a while and then write. The things he writes all will be concentrated toward one point: warmth. While he's writing, he also wants to play experimentally with small groups. Ideally, he'd like to spend six months a year in France and six months here.

"'You've got to do it that way,' he explains. "You've got to be here for the commercial things and in France for relaxing facilities.'

"Relaxation is something Charlie constantly has missed. Lack of relaxation, he thinks, has spoiled most of the records he has made. To hear him tell it, he has never cut a good side. Some of the things he did on the Continental label he considered more relaxed than the rest. But every record he has made could stand improvement, he says. We tried to pin him down, to get him to name a few sides that were at least better than the rest.

"'Suppose a guy came up to us,' we said, 'and said, "I've got four bucks and I want to buy three Charlie Parker records. What'll I buy?" What should we tell him?'

"'Tell him to keep his money,' he said."

And in a radio interview with me in Boston in 1953 Bird was on the same kick. "Everytime I hear a record I've made," he said, "I hear all kinds of things I could improve on, things I should have done. There's always so much more to be done in music. It's so vast."

That same evening, Charlie amplified further on some of his plans: "I'd like to do a session with five or six woodwinds, a harp, a choral group, and full rhythm section. Something on the line of Hindemith's *Kleine Kammermusik*. Not a copy or anything like that. I don't want ever to copy. But that sort of thing."

He also talked of other classical music he liked. I have no way of knowing how intimately he knew these works, but I can testify that he spoke with a strength of emotion that could not have been entirely put on. Or maybe, being Bird, it could have. Anyway, this is what he said: "I first began listening seven or eight years ago. First I heard Stravinsky's *Firebird Suite*. In the vernacular of the streets, I flipped. I guess Bartok has become my favorite. I dig all the moderns. And also the classical men, Bach, Beethoven, etc.

"It's a funny thing, listening to music, any kind," Bird went on. "What you hear depends on so many things in yourself. Like I heard Bartok's *Second Piano Concerto* over here, and later I heard it again in France. I was more acclimated to life then, and I heard things in it I never heard before. You never know what's going to happen when you listen to music. All kinds of things can suddenly open up."

In many ways Bird was a protean master of the put-on, including, of course, his ability to put himself on. But there is no question that, when he wasn't obsessed elsewhere, Bird found music to be the only element of his life which gave him some realistic promise that all kinds of things *could* suddenly open up.

On the other hand, for all the adulation he eventually received from hordes of younger musicians, he was insecure more often than not because he strongly sensed, I think, that he had only fulfilled part of his potential, maybe only a small part, and he did not know how to make the next leap. Bird did not have, to say the least, the discipline that John Coltrane relentlessly exercised in his last years, a discipline by which Coltrane kept forcing himself to dig deeper and deeper into his resources, his potential, while adding to those resources.

Bird was too often on the run. He could almost always blow, but reflection and study were something else. Something else he could never get together. Gigi Gryce, an alto saxophonist and a friend of Bird, recalled after Parker's death: "Charlie used to get very depressed when he couldn't execute all the things he wanted to. He felt he hadn't even gotten started as to what he *could* have done. He often said he'd failed in his music."

He hadn't failed, of course. Bird turned jazz around, as Louis and Duke had before him, and Coltrane was to afterward. But he could have gone farther and he knew that.

Bird really did marvel, in his way, at the myriad pleasures in music, all kinds of music. Once, at a musicians' bar, Bird insisted on playing some country music recordings on the jukebox. He had no patience with the jibes of other jazzmen present that these were the corniest of sounds. "No," Bird insisted, "they're telling stories that are real to them. I hear what they're saying."

Or, as Gigi Gryce put it: "Bird loved just about anyone who played." And Billie Wallington, wife of pianist George Wallington and currently an executive at Warner Brothers Records, remembers: "A few weeks before his death, Bird was walking along Broadway with just fifty cents in his pocket. He met a blind beggar who was playing the accordion. Bird dropped a quarter into the blind man's bowl and asked him if he'd play *All the Things You Are*. A few minutes later, Parker walked by the accordionist again and the latter was still playing the same song. Charlie laughed and said to the person with him, 'This guy plays the right chords.' He then took his last twenty-five cents out of the pocket of his old pants and gave them to the blind man."

The late Dave Lambert, who had known Bird very well, said: "He had experienced everything in his life except peace." Whose fault was that? And another musician, Teddy Blume, who managed Bird for a time, said that being with Charlie Parker over a long period was like "having a terrible disease." Whose fault was that?

To some, it was our fault. Society's fault. Kenneth Rexroth saw Bird and Dylan Thomas, "the heroes of the postwar generation," as having been "overcome by the horror of the world in which they found themselves, because at last they could no longer overcome that world with the weapon of a purely lyrical art."

In Ross Russell's biography of Bird, pianist Hampton Hawes ascribed Bird's long plunge to destruction to "how deeply he felt about racism." Unaware of the strong black consciousness of Duke Ellington, Rex Stewart, Lester

Young, Frankie Newton, and hundreds more jazzmen who preceded Bird, Hawes said of Parker that "he was the first jazz musician I met who understood what was happening to his people. He couldn't come up with an answer. So he stayed high."

Ross Russell himself appears to believe that Bird, being black in a white society, was foredoomed: "In spite of his successes and growing prestige, Charlie saw no future for the music he played, or for his race in America. To live once, and to the limit—that was his game plan."

Bird believed some of that himself. When Babs Gonzales, the singer and antic entrepreneur, tried to persuade Parker to get off drugs, Bird's answer was: "Wait until everybody gets rich off your style and you don't have any bread, then lecture me about drugs."

Yet notwithstanding the pervasive racism in America, including the jazz business, the death-of-Bird-at-the-hands-of-society is too simplistic a conclusion. His bitterness and many of his wounds were caused by racism, and his fundamental insularity may well have had part of its base in racism. ("I don't let anyone get close to me," Bird once said to a man who thought himself a close friend. "Even you. Or my wife.")

But why did others survive? Dizzy Gillespie, Duke Ellington, Cecil Taylor? I don't know and I doubt if anybody else really does. But just as there is no quick, easy way to explain Bird's astonishing creativity, so there is no instant explanation of his greatly premature extinction. More than any critic or biographer, it would more likely be a novelist, a black novelist, who might eventually illuminate those parts of the cold inner darkness that finally took over all of Bird.

Duke Jordan recalls, "As years went by, Bird started cooling. He went to a doctor in 1948 and was told he had about six months to live unless he took a complete rest for a few years, which he never did. His ulcers were bad, and his whole body was filled with a terrible cold."

There have been many tragic figures in jazz, but perhaps none was so rudderless, so beset by hellhounds on his trail, than Bird. And some of those hellhounds had his face.

Once, near the end of his life, on a street in Greenwich Village in front of a night club, Charlie Parker ordered one of his protégés, Jackie McLean: "I want you to kick me in the ass." McLean kept refusing and Bird kept insisting. "I want you to kick me in the ass for letting me get myself in this position."

Finally, McLean obeyed Bird's command. "Don't you ever allow this to happen to *you*," Bird said to him.

Bird knew it wasn't only "they" who had destroyed him. But he never knew how he could keep himself from helping "them" to destroy him. All the other changes he knew, but not that one.

jazz is:

The listener. **Gil Evans** and I had met on the street and we started talking about a new jazz composition. I told him I was not well-enough trained musically to analyze the work properly.

"But I thought you knew better than that," Gil said. "The listener—and obviously, he's the one all us musicians are trying to reach—doesn't have to be able to 'analyze.' He doesn't necessarily have to know how it's put together. But if we *can* reach him emotionally, he becomes part of the music. He adds his responses to the continuum of experience that keeps alive what a musician does. I mean, the music is out there, becoming part of so many different people's experiences, affecting so many different kinds of consciousnesses in ways the musician can't possibly conceive. Reaching is what counts, not the listener's ability to analyze."

John Coltrane, as I interview him for the notes to one of his albums, saying: "The music has to speak for itself. I'd much rather you didn't put anything technical in the notes. It might get in the way of people finding out what there is in the music for them."

Billie Holiday, remembering Lester Young: "Everyone, when he first started, thought: This man, his *tone* is too *thin*, you know? A tenor sax! Everybody thinks it has to be real big; and Lester used to go out of his mind getting reeds to sound *big*, like Chu Berry (he was very popular in those days). And I told Lester, 'It doesn't *matter* because,' I said, 'you have a *beautiful* tone and you *watch*. After a while *everybody's* going to be *copying* you.' And it came to *be*.'"

Jimmy Giuffre, in J.C. Thomas' book, *Chasin' the Trane*: "When I first heard Coltrane with Miles, he sounded ugly to me. I'm from the Lester Young school of subtle, mellow intonation, and I prefer brevity in my solos. John's reedy, raspy sound and extended solos turned me off at first. But I kept listening to him, because his ideas were so advanced. Eventually I got used to his sound and I began to understand that his bold, flat statements were as if he was standing naked on stage, the music coming directly from the man, not the horn. Later I heard hundreds of other tenor players emulating him, copying him note for note. Sometimes I feel like saying, there is only *one* John Coltrane; you should listen and learn from him and otherwise let him be."

express trane

John Coltrane

Art Blakey

Coltrane, a man of almost unbelievable gentleness made human to us lesser mortals by his very occasional rages. Coltrane, an authentically spiritual man, but not innocent of carnal imperatives. Or perhaps more accurately, a man, in his last years, especially but not exclusively consumed by affairs of the spirit. That is, having constructed a personal world view (or view of the cosmos) on a residue of Christianity and an infusion of Eastern meditative practices and concerns, Coltrane became a theosophist of jazz. The music was a way of self-purgation so that he could learn more about himself to the end of making himself and his music part of the unity of all being. He truly believed this, and in this respect, as well as musically, he has been a powerful influence on many musicians since. He considered music to be a healing art, an "uplifting" art.

Yet through most of his most relatively short career (he died at forty), Coltrane divided jazz listeners, creating furiously negative reactions to his work among some. ("Antijazz" was one of the epithets frequently cast at him in print.) He was hurt and somewhat bewildered by this reaction, but with monumental stubbornness went on exploring and creating what to many seemed at first to be chaos—self-indulgent, long-winded noise. Some still think that's what it was.

Others believed Coltrane to be a prophet, a musical prophet, heralding an enormous expansion of what it might now be possible to say on an instrument. Consider Art Davis. He is a startlingly brilliant bassist, as accomplished in classical music as in jazz. (Because Davis is black, he has been denied employment by those symphony orchestras to which he has applied, and so he has challenged them to pit him against any classical bassist of their choice. The challenge has gone unanswered.) Anyway, Davis, whom I've known for years, is a rationalist, a keen analyzer of music and of life. He is not given, so far as I have ever known, to giant or even small leaps into faith. Davis requires a sound scaffolding of fact and proof for his enthusiasms.

But here is Art Davis, who played for a time with Coltrane, as quoted in the Fall 1972 issue of the periodical *Black Creation* [Institute of Afro-American Affairs at New York University]: "John Coltrane would play for hours a set. One tune would be like an hour or two hours, and he would not repeat himself, and it would not be boring . . . . People would just be shouting, like you go to church, a holy roller church or something like that. This would get into their brains, would penetrate. John had that spirit—he was after the spiritual thing. . . . You could hear people screaming . . . despite the critics who tried to put him down. Black people made him because they stuck together and they saw—look what's going down—let's get some of this. You know all the hard times that John had at the beginning, even when he was with Miles. And when he left Miles, starting out, everybody tried to discourage him. But I'd be there and the brothers and sisters would be there and they supported him. . . . John had this power of communication, that power so rare it was like genius—I'll call him a prophet because he did this."

Coltrane had another power, a power of self-regeneration that also has to do with that power of communication. One evening in the early 1950's, I saw Coltrane in Sheridan Square, in Greenwich Village. He looked awful. Raggedy, vacant. "Junk," said a musician with me. "He's been hooked a while." But, I noted, he had a bottle of wine in his hand. "That, too," said the musician.

And Coltrane stopped using both. By himself. During his huge musical ascent, which was soon to start. Coltrane was clean and stayed clean. That's power. Like Miles.

Coltrane changed jazz in as fundamental a way as Charlie Parker had before him and Louis Armstrong before Parker. One thing he did was to radically reshape—by the overwhelming persuasiveness of his playing—all previous jazz definitions of "acceptable" sounds and forms.

Obviously, through the decades, jazz had encompassed an extraordinary range of sounds—growls, slurs, cries, guffaws, keening wails. And certainly it had been accepted from the beginning that each player had his own "sound." There was never any one criterion for how every trombone or tenor saxophone or singer should sound. Still, at each stage of jazz history certain kinds of sounds were beyond the pale. Or at least they were considerably downgraded. For years, to cite a pre-modern-jazz example, Pee Wee Russell's rasping tone (which, to its denigrators, veered between a squeak and an access of laryngitis) was mocked by a good many musicians as well as listeners. Yet Pee Wee proved to be among the most inventive and seizingly original of all clarinetists.

Lester Young was in disfavor among some of his peers for quite a while because his sound was too "light" compared to Coleman Hawkins' robust fullness. Nor was Lee Wiley the only appraiser to think of Billie Holiday that she sounded "as if her shoes were too tight." At the advent of Charlie Parker one of the many criticisms of his playing by older musicians and by traditionalist listeners was that his tone was "bad," too acrid by contrast, say, with that of Johnny Hodges.

In the case of John Coltrane, a majority of the initial reviews of his recordings in the early and mid-1950's also cited his "strident," "unpleasant" sound. Mine were among them. Later, however, when Coltrane was really underway and pushing his instrument beyond any previous limits of sound possibilities, the intermittent rawness of his tone, the high-pitched squeals, the braying yawps, the screams, generated even more intense hostility along with the denunciation that his extensive solos were structureless, directionless. "Musical nonsense" wrote one critic.

In retrospect, however, it is clear that Coltrane was one of the most persistent, relentless expanders of possibility—all kinds of possibility: textural, emotional, harmonic, and spiritual—in jazz history. And also one of the most totally exposed improvisers in the history of the music.

I was converted, or educated, from listening first to Coltrane with Miles Davis for many nights. This was the Coltrane "sheets of sound" period (a phrase originated by critic Ira Gitler). The term came about, Gitler later explained, "because of the density of textures he was using. His multinote improvisations were so thick and complex they were almost flowing out of the horn by themselves. That really hit me, the continuous flow of ideas without stopping. It was almost superhuman, and the amount of energy he was using could have powered a spaceship."

Miles would sometimes grumble about the constant hailstorms of notes in a Coltrane solo, since Miles himself preferred to work with space, to let his notes breathe. And the length of the solos also occasionally annoyed him. "Why did you go on so long?" he once asked Coltrane after a particularly lengthy flight by the latter.

"It took that long to get it all in," said Coltrane, and Miles accepted the logic of the answer.

Actually, Miles Davis was much intrigued by the sheer will to creativity of Coltrane on his better nights. "Coltrane's really something," Miles told me one afternoon in

1958. "He's been working on those arpeggios and playing them fifty different ways and playing them all at once. However," there was a glint of triumph in Miles, "he *is* beginning to leave more space—except when he gets nervous."

It was important for Coltrane to work with Miles. For one thing, of course, he received attention, with the Davis imprimatur legitimatizing Coltrane for some of those who up to that point had considered Trane either incompetent or a charlatan or both. Miles, it was agreed by nearly all, could not and would not be conned musically. If he hired the man, the man must have something to say. That imprimatur also gave Coltrane confidence. Feeling set upon by the critics, he had passed a far more severe test by being considered worthy of a place in the Miles Davis band.

Even more valuable to Coltrane, however, was his stay with Thelonious Monk—in between stints with Miles Davis in the late 1950's. That collaboration at the Five Spot Café in New York's East Village was a key historic event—of the musical order of Louis Armstrong playing second cornet to King Oliver at the Royal Garden Café in Chicago in the 1920's. I was there nearly every night all the weeks Monk and Trane played the Five Spot, and it was there I finally understood how nonpareil a musician, how dauntless an explorer Coltrane was. The excitement was so heady that soon musicians were standing two and three deep at the bar of the Five Spot nearly every night.

Monk creates a total musical microcosm, and for musicians who play with him the challenge is to keep your balance, to stay with Monk, no matter where his unpredictably intricate imagination leads—and at the same time, play yourself, be yourself.

"I learned new levels of alertness with Monk," Coltrane said, "because if you didn't keep aware all the time of what was going on, you'd suddenly feel as if you'd stepped into a hole without a bottom to it." He learned other things as well. "Monk was one of the first to show me how to make two or three notes at one time on tenor. It's done by false fingering and adjusting your lips, and if it's done right you get triads. He also got me into the habit of playing long solos [longer than with Miles] on his pieces, playing the same piece for a long time to find new conceptions for solos. It got so I would go as far as possible on one phrase until I ran out of ideas. The harmonies got to be an obsession for me. Sometimes I was making music through the wrong end of a magnifying glass."

As a teacher, one of the most liberating teachers in jazz, Monk had another kind of impact on Coltrane, as on practically all the musicians who have played with him. Monk kept insisting that musicians must keep working at stretching themselves, at going beyond their limitations, which really were artificial limitations that came from their having absorbed conventional—and thereby gratutitously constricting—standards of what can and what cannot be done on an instrument.

Before Coltrane came with the band, Gigi Gryce had learned this lesson: "I had a part Monk wrote for me that was impossible. I had to play melody while simultaneously playing harmony with him. In addition, the intervals were very wide besides; and I just told him I couldn't do it. 'You have an instrument, don't you?' he said. 'Either play it or throw it away.' And he walked away. Finally, I *was* able to play it. Another time I was orchestrating a number for him, and I didn't write everything down for the horns exactly as he'd outlined it because I felt the musicians would look at the score and figure it was impossible to play. He was very angry, and he finally got exactly what he wanted. I remember the trumpet player on the date had some runs going up on his horn and Monk said they were only impractical if they didn't give him a chance to breathe. The range was not a factor 'because a man should be flexible on all ranges of his horn.' "

Then came Coltrane. The story, told by Art Blakey, is in J.C. Thomas' *Chasin' The Trane:* "I played drums on the *Monk's Music* album for Riverside, where Monk expanded his group to a septet with both Coleman Hawkins and John Coltrane on tenor. Naturally, Monk wrote all the music, but Hawk was having trouble reading it, so he asked Monk to explain it to both Trane and himself. Monk said to Hawk, 'You're the great Coleman Hawkins, right? You're the guy who invented the tenor saxophone, right?' Hawk agreed. Then Monk turned to Trane, 'You're the great John Coltrane, right?' Trane blushed, and mumbled, 'Aw . . . I'm not so great.' Then Monk said to both of them, 'You play saxophone, right?' They nodded. 'Well, the music is on the horn. Between the two of you, you should be able to find it.' "

. Coltrane kept looking and finding, and, never satisfied, looked some more. His audience was growing, especially among musicians, but more nonmusicians were finding that if they *actively* listened to his music, their whole way of hearing jazz might well be changed. This did not mean, however, that they had to listen analytically. In the liner notes for Coltrane's album, *Om,* for example, I suggested that those who were finding Coltrane "difficult" start again, but this time without "worrying about how it is all structured, where it's leading. Let the music come in without any pre-set definitions of what jazz *has* to be, of what *music* has to be.

"If you find yourself responding—and I don't mean necessarily with conventional 'pleasure,' but rather with any strong feeling—listen on. In this music, just as textures are themselves shapes and motion is by colors as well as by time"; so, in the listening, I should have gone on, ingress is by routes that will unexpectedly come upon you in guises other than the usual ways to get into a piece of music. A link of pitches perhaps, an a-rhythmic phrase that will lead to a strong subterranean pulsation.

For the last seven years of his life Coltrane continued to make more demands of himself musically than any jazz musician, except perhaps Cecil Taylor, ever has. None of this, so far as I could tell, was done as an act of competition. It was himself, and only himself, Coltrane kept pressuring to hear more, feel more, understand more, communicate more. At home he would practice for hours, sometimes silently—just running his fingers over the keys—and pick up new instruments and meditate and listen to recordings of Indian music and the music of South African Pygmies. Possibilities. Always more possibilities. He decided he wanted two drummers working with him. Then, on an album, he fixed on two bass players. I asked him why. "Because I want more of the sense of the expansion of time. I want the time to be more plastic."

Time. Vast, fierce stretches of time. The music sometimes sounding like the exorcism of a multitude of demons, each one of whom was mightily resisting his expulsion. Yet at other times Coltrane could sound his probes with such gentle luminescence as to fool the voracious spirits, but soon the shaking, smashing, endless battle would begin again.

At night clubs there were scores, hundreds of exhilarating, exhausting nights during which the listeners, along with the musicians, had no resting space but had to keep emotional pace as best he could with the ferociously wheeling, diving, climbing Coltrane.

For better or worse, and that depended on the inventiveness of the musicians who followed him, Coltrane more than any other player legitimated the extended jazz solo. As Archie Shepp, a tenor saxophonist befriended and influenced by Coltrane, said, "That was his breakthrough—the concept that the imperatives of conception might make it necessary to improvise at great length. I don't mean he proved that a thirty- or forty-minute solo is necessarily better than a three-minute one. He did prove, however, that it was possible to create thirty or forty minutes of uninterrupted, continually building, continually original and imaginative music. And in the process, Coltrane also showed the rest of us we had to have the stamina—in terms of imagination and physical preparedness—to sustain those long flights."

I once tried out on Coltrane my theory that one reason he developed such long solos was in an attempt to create and sustain a kind of hypnotic, dervishlike mood so that the listener would in time become oblivious to distractions and end up wholly immersed in the music with all his customary intellectual and emotional defenses removed.

"That may be a secondary effect," Coltrane said, "but I'm not consciously trying to do that. I'm still primarily looking into certain sounds, certain scales. Not that I'm sure of what I'm looking for, except that it'll be something that hasn't been played before. I don't know what it is. I know I'll have that feeling when I get it. And in the process of looking, continual looking, the result in any given performance can be long or short. I never know. It's always one thing leading into another. It keeps evolving, and sometimes it's longer than I actually thought it was while I was playing. When things are constantly happening the piece just doesn't feel that long."

Always looking, Coltrane always tried to be ready for

the unexpected revelation, "that feeling." Alice Coltrane told me that "when John left for work he'd often take five instruments with him. He wanted to be ready for whatever came. That was characteristic of John. His music was never resigned, never complacent. How could it be? He never stopped surprising himself."

He was a man who spoke of universal, transcendent peace—becoming one with Om, "the first vibration—that sound, that spirit which set everything else into being." And yet his music, to the end, although sometimes almost eerily serene, remained most often volcanic. Ravi Shankar, who had come to know Coltrane, said: "I was much disturbed by his music. Here was a creative person who had become a vegetarian, who was studying yoga and reading the *Bhagavad-Gita,* yet in whose music I still heard much turmoil. I could not understand it."

Marion Brown, the alto saxophonist and composer, was one of the musicians assembled by Coltrane for his almost unbearably intense set of "free jazz," *Ascension,* and Brown recalls: "We did two takes, and they both had that kind of thing in them that makes people scream. The people in the studios were screaming."

Perhaps Om, the first vibration, is a scream. Perhaps Coltrane wished so hard to transcend all of what he regarded as his baser, antispiritual elements, that he was doomed, from the time his ambition became so otherworldly, to always feel desperately imprisoned. Hence the scream. But part of the scream may also have been the pain, the difficulty, of self-purgation, a process that had become the normative conundrum of thorns in his life.

Whatever the explanation—if there is a discernible matrix of explanations for the phenomenon of Coltrane—by the time he died of cancer of the liver in 1967, he had helped shape a new generation of jazz musicians. He didn't like the term "jazz," by the way, since he felt all music to be one, without labels.

In musical terms Trane's contributions have perhaps been most succinctly described by David Baker, who has long taught black music, and other music, at the University of Indiana. Now that Grove's *Dictionary of Music and Musicians* has at last decided to admit articles on jazz musicians, Baker is writing an entry on, among others, John Coltrane. And the achievements of Coltrane he will cite are: "using multiphonics, playing several notes or tones simultaneously; creating asymmetrical groupings not dependent on the basic pulse; developing an incredibly sophisticated system of chord substitutions; and initiating a pan-modal style of playing, using several modes simultaneously. I've transcribed some of his solos for teaching my students at the University of Indiana. I think all musicians should study Coltrane solos the way we now study the études of Bach and Brahms."

Coltrane, who read theory as well as biographies of the creative (Van Gogh, for instance), might have been pleased to hear that. But at night, on the stand, there would be no abiding satisfaction for him in what he had done in the past. "You just keep going," he told me once. "You keep trying to get right down to the crux."

He even frustrated himself—in addition to knowing the crux would always be beyond him or anyone else—by yearning for yet another impossibility. "Sometimes," Coltrane said to me one afternoon, "I wish I could walk up to my music as if for the first time, as if I had never heard it before. Being so inescapably a part of it, I'll never know what the listener gets, what the listener feels, and that's too bad."

Looking at Coltrane's early background—born in Hamlet, North Carolina; schooling in Philadelphia; rhythm-and-blues work with Eddie "Mr. Cleanhead" Vinson; gathering experience with Dizzy Gillespie, Earl Bostic, Johnny Hodges, Miles Davis, and Thelonious Monk—there would have been no way to predict (before Miles and Monk, anyway) the singular, unyieldingly questioning force that was to revolutionize much of jazz. There never is any way to predict the coming of the next jazz prophet. And that's why nearly all speculation, learned or otherwise, about the future directions of jazz is always futile. The future of jazz has always depended on unexpected individuals with radical (though at first seemingly opaque) questions to ask—questions they eventually proceed to answer: Louis Armstrong on the nature of the jazz solo; Duke Ellington on the nature of the jazz orchestra; Charlie Parker on the obsolescence of the rhythmic and harmonic language that preceded him; and John Coltrane on all manner of jazz constrictions that antedated *him*.

In spending himself on trying to answer the questions that consumed him, Coltrane eventually developed what in jazz terms could be called a large audience. As Martin Williams has pointed out, "It was almost impossible for a man to be as much of a technician, artist, and explorer as Coltrane and still have the kind of popular following he had. What did he tell that audience? In what new and meaningful things did his music instruct them?

"I don't know, of course," Williams continued. "And perhaps as a white man I can't know. But I would venture a suggestion. I don't think Coltrane spoke of society or political theory. I think that like all real artists he spoke of matters of the spirit, of those things by which the soul of man survives. I think he spoke of the ways of the demons and the gods that were always there, yet are always contemporary. And I think that he knew that he did."

Some months after Coltrane died, I was visiting a black college in Delaware. It had been a year during which I had lectured at many colleges—mostly on education and civil liberties. When music had come into the discussion, the emphasis invariably was on rock sounds and players. Only at this black college did the students talk of Bird and Ornette Coleman, and especially of Coltrane.

"You know," one of the black students said, "when Trane died, it was like a great big hole had been left. And it's still there."

In one sense that hole is indeed still there and will continue to be. Obviously, certain artists do leave great big holes when they die, for they are irreplaceable in the size and scope of their originality. Louis Armstrong. Duke. Lester Young. Coleman Hawkins. Billie Holiday. And on and on. As this book is being written, there has yet been no successor to Coltrane in terms of having dominant, pervasive influence on the jazz of the 1970's.

On the other hand, as pianist Keith Jarrett said of Trane's death, "Everyone felt a big gap all of a sudden. But he didn't intend to leave a gap. He intended that there be more space for everybody to do what they should do."

And there *is* more space for further generations of seekers. In one way or another they are all children of Coltrane. And, of course, of all those who shaped him. The legacy is long and rich and demanding.

jazz is:

Louis Armstrong, in the early years of modern jazz, not smiling, contemptuous, saying of what Charlie Parker and Dizzy Gillespie were playing: "That's got nothing to do with jazz. That's Chinese music."

"Pops is the greatest, right?" a musician said, at the time, outside of Armstrong's hearing. "He is the greatest at what *he* does. So that's jazz to him. What's coming up now he doesn't understand, so he puts it down."

Ornette Coleman, his first engagement in New York, at the Five Spot in the late fall of 1959, coming off the stand and saying to me, "I thought it would be different in New York. I thought the musicians here were more serious. But it's just like everywhere else. Most of them are so hostile. What they don't understand they hate."

A few weeks later, **Roy Eldridge,** shaking his head, said to me about Coleman's music: "I listened to him all kinds of ways. I listened to him high and I listened to him cold sober. I even played with him. I think he's jiving, baby. He's putting everybody on. They start with a nice lead-off figure, but then they go off into outer space. They disregard the chords and they play odd numbers of bars. I can't follow them."

Stories I kept hearing about **Cecil Taylor** during
the 1950's at musicians' bars. How one night Jo
Jones, who had been steaming ever since Taylor sat
in on piano, finally erupted, throwing his top
cymbal across the room. How other musicians, at
other sessions, had expressed similar anger and
disdain. Like what happened one Monday night at
Birdland where Cecil was playing, and among
those in the audience were Miles Davis, Dizzy
Gillespie, and Sarah Vaughan. "Miles just cursed
and walked out," Cecil told A.B. Spellman in *Four
Lives in the Bebop Business*. "Dizzy wandered in
and out and kept making all kinds of remarks to
Sarah, who was in a pretty vicious mood. Miles
later put me down in print."

A club owner in New York in the mid-1960's: "I'm
not going to hire that Taylor again. That's not
music. That's noise. And he plays so goddamn
hard he knocks my piano out of whack. Whoever
told him he was a musician, way back, sure did
him a bad turn."

Buell Neidlinger, Cecil Taylor's bassist during the
hardest years, recalling: "We once played a club
and after about eight bars of Cecil's piano the
owner came running up and told us to get out of
the club. He wouldn't even let us finish one song."

cecil taylor's spirit-music

Cecil Taylor

Thelonious Monk

In jazz, as in any form of expression, the developers of new forms, new language, new colors, new ways of hearing, seeing, feeling—they are nearly always regarded at first with suspicion or scorn or even hatred, laughed at, put in Coventry, treated as fools and fakers.

In jazz no one was so persistently treated as a pariah for so long as Cecil Taylor. But it didn't work. By the mid-1970's Taylor had finally emerged as being of the stature, in his way, of Thelonious Monk and John Coltrane. Not on the level of Duke Ellington, but this is a level so far occupied only by Duke.

In a 1975 interview with the Canadian jazz magazine, *Coda*, Cecil Taylor was telling of an evening, twenty years before, when he first saw Carmen Amaya dance: "It was as though everything stopped for me. I mean everything *stopped*. That, to me, is the highest kind of compliment that can be paid to another artist—to make somebody else lose all sense of time, all sense of his own existence outside [of the performance]."

That is also what Cecil Taylor does to people. That is, to those listeners who are willing to hear beyond what they have known and who are not afraid of the enormous emotional demands Taylor makes on them and on himself. There is continuous intellectual fascination in the furious storms of improvisatory structures he creates; but the typhoonlike power of Taylor's music is, above all, that of heavy energy, heavy feeling. It can all be analyzed, but that's not its point. As Taylor says, "Part of what this music is about is not to be delineated exactly. It's about magic, and capturing spirits."

I have been drawn to that magic for more than twenty years, having first heard Taylor when he was a student in Boston in the early 1950's. During that decade too he disturbed, he almost frightened, listeners. Not all of them. A few musicians were aware of his powers, and a very few critics. One of the latter was Whitney Balliett, who reported on an extraordinary Taylor performance at the Great South Bay Festival outside New York City in 1958. Balliett described how part of the audience "fidgeted, whispered and wandered nervously in and out of the tent, as if the ground beneath had become unbearably hot."

On the other hand, at the same concert there were those, including Balliett, who listened in no little wonder at such prodigies of torrential invention. And when it was over, as I wrote at the time, "a nucleus of intensely attentive listeners ran—I mean, ran—to the stand to find out whether any of his records were available."

What mesmerized the small minority then, and the ever larger number of listeners now, is the overwhelming energy of the man's music. It is an energy of ideas, of multiple intersecting rhythm waves, of textures and timbres, of structures and emotions. And there is also the driving sense of constant building, a phantasmagoria of dynamics. Everything—structures, feelings, rhythms—move up and through space in bristlingly, careeningly interconnected patterns until the closing climax (after many previous ones), which is felt, however, not as a definitive ending but rather as a pause in the history of Cecil Taylor's music. As Duke Ellington said, no music ever ends.

Yet another element of Taylor is his relentless pushing, stretching, almost rending of possibility. As Balliett wrote in 1975: "He has become obsessed with blocks of sound, with sequoias of sound, and if he could not produce on the piano what he hears in his head, he would do it by other means. He would gather about him whales and jets and cascades, and make them sing and roar and crash. And we'd listen."

Cecil Taylor was born in Long Island City on March 15, 1933, and grew up in Corona, Long Island. His mother (whose own mother was an Indian) played violin and piano, and his father, a chef, was immersed in black folklore. "He could talk about how it was with the slaves in the 1860's," Taylor told A.B. Spellman, "about the field shouts and hollers, about myths of black people." The elder Taylor sang, not only the blues but, as Cecil said to me some years ago, "things that go back farther than the blues."

There was always music in the house, and Duke Ellington's work was particularly respected by Taylor's parents. The youngster resisted Ellington at first ("I always made it a point to disagree with the family"), but gradually became influenced by Duke. "In a sense, I've never thought 'pianistically,'" Taylor says, "because I think of the piano as an orchestra. For a long time I didn't particularly dig what they call pianists, because they weren't using the piano fully. Then I began to really hear Ellington and Fats Waller, and I realized how orchestral jazz-piano playing could be."

Another thing Taylor learned from Ellington, as he told A. B. Spellman, is that "you can make the group you play with sing if you realize each of the instruments has a distinctive personality; and you can bring out the singing aspect of that personality if you use the right timbre for the instrument."

After high school, Cecil studied piano, composition, and harmony at the New York College of Music and then at the New England Conservatory in Boston. I got to know him there, attended concerts with him, and continually learned from him, because Cecil then as now was critically curious about all kinds of music. Also, then as now, he was so attuned to what was truly advanced in music that he never acted as if he had to prove his hipness. His authority was in his taste.

For some years thereafter Taylor was sometimes criticized because there were discernible elements of European music—Bartok, for instance—in his own work. In recent years, as Taylor has developed further, there are fewer such traces, but his comment at the time is sharply illustrative of his approach to his art as a black musician. In 1958 Taylor told me: "I am not afraid of European influences. The point is to use them—as Ellington did—as part of my life as an American Negro. Some people say I'm atonal. It depends, for one thing, on your definition of the term. In any case, it depends on the musicians I come up with. Basically, it's not important whether a certain chord happens to fit some student's definition of atonality. A man like Thelonious Monk, for example, is concerned with growing and enriching his musical conception, and *what he does comes as a living idea out of his life's experience, not from a theory*. It may or may not turn out to be atonal. Similarly, as Miles Davis's European technical facility becomes sparser, his comment from the Negro folk tradition becomes more incisive. He's been an important innovator in form in jazz, but again *not out of theory, but out of what he hears and lives*." [Emphasis added. N.H.]

And the life and cultural roots of a black musician obviously are different from those of a white musician. Accordingly, it is absurd to evaluate the technique of a Thelonious Monk by criteria associated with Vladimir Horowitz. Each wants to say quite different things, and those expressions require quite different techniques. And in that division is part of the essence of jazz—going back to those early brass players in the South during the latter part of the nineteenth century who themselves created the techniques they needed to play the blues and other prejazz sounds going back to work songs, hollers, and other black life experiences. So it is that Cecil Taylor, as A. B. Spellman has noted, "finds it no disadvantage that Ornette Coleman taught himself violin in a manner that would never satisfy a competent violin teacher: 'Cats said to me, "Well, you know Ornette doesn't know much about the violin." I said, "What do you mean?" "Well, he couldn't play like Heifetz!".... But, in spite of Heifetz's great technique, he has never come up with a sound like Ornette. He has never played the music that Ornette plays on the violin.'"

In Cecil Taylor's playing there is no question any longer that his formidable command of the instrument is essentially based on a black technique coming out of what he hears and lives as a black man. A key element in that technique, by the way, is the dance. As long as I've known him Taylor has been intrigued by various dance forms. "I try to imitate on piano the leaps in space a dancer makes," he has said. But there's more to it than that. Like Thelonious Monk, Taylor sometimes uses his feet and body like a dancer when he plays. Bassist Buell Neidlinger noticed this during his early association as a sideman with Taylor: "He does things with a speed that most pianists, if they heard it on a record, would say, 'How does he do that?' It has a lot to do with the rhythmic flailing of his arms or his ability to move his body back and forth like a pendulum from one end of the piano to the other so that he can put his hands in the proper position, and I think his interest in the dance has a lot to do with that."

While Taylor has become knowledgeable about all kinds of dance, black dancers—particularly the late Baby Laurence, the most brilliantly, precisely inventive of all the jazz dancers—have had the most powerful impact on him.

As for his career, once he left the New England Conservatory of Music Taylor was learning all he could about black music, gradually losing interest in those white musicians, such as Dave Brubeck, whose harmonic density had earlier interested him. Briefly he worked with Hot Lips Page and Johnny Hodges, among others, but for a long time jobs at music were so scarce that he had to work at what he could get by day—cook, dishwasher, record salesman, delivery man for a coffee shop.

During one period, when he had not played before an audience for more than six months, Cecil told me that when he practiced in his room he played as if he were in front of an audience. "I have to make that imaginative leap, I have to believe I'm communicating to somebody, I have to keep the contact going."

We had been talking on the street, and watching him walk away I saw in his very walk no lessening of that almost awesome, almost terrifying determination to become what he wanted to be that I had first seen in Boston when he was a student.

It took many years. There were some relatively prestigious European engagements before he really began to break through in America; and for several years he taught and developed orchestras at various universities. He taught hard and long, demanding, as usual, as much of his students as he had always demanded of his sidemen and of himself. At last, by 1974, he had found his audience, or rather it had found him, for he was continuing to forge his music in his own uncompromising, fiercely kinetic way.

Writing of a 1974 Cecil Taylor engagement in New York at a club whose owner had once sworn never to hire him again, Whitney Balliett marveled: "Cecil Taylor packing them into the Five Spot for three solid weeks! Cecil Taylor playing *encores* to get off the stand! Cecil Taylor—iconoclast, super-avant-gardist, mysterioso pianist—a matinee idol! Incredible but true."

Of the current incredible but true Cecil Taylor, Buell Neidlinger, who has played for a number of prestigious symphony orchestras and chamber groups, says: "That man is capable of playing ten different notes with ten different fingers, ten different dynamics, ten different attacks, and at ten different tempi. He is phenomenal. There is no musician I've met, including Igor Stravinsky and Pierre Boulez, who comes anywhere near having the abilities that Cecil Taylor has. He has now fully developed his materials. He has never copied anyone. He is a product of his own genius."

Cecil is also an exemplar of a way of playing and hearing that was once concisely described by a musician who burst into a Charles Mingus rehearsal years ago, urgently intent on telling Minus of a new tenor player, Booker Ervin, whom he had just heard. "That cat," the musician shouted, "cuts just about everybody. He doesn't play just notes and changes; he plays *music*."

So too Cecil Taylor. In 1958, in the first extensive analysis of Taylor's music, Gunther Schuller pointed out, as Martin Williams noted in a later essay on Taylor, that Cecil "at his most adventurous . . . was never arbitrary but simply letting the force and logic of a musical idea carry him and . . . like Thelonious Monk, Taylor plays passages in which the overall musical shape and direction takes precedent over the actual notes. The choice of notes is secondary to the larger musical contours."

Notes on a page, musical designs on a page, no matter how avant-garde they purportedly are, are seen by Taylor to be what he calls "dead music"—by contrast with notes as transmuted, in improvisatory action, by jazz musicians. "When you ask a man to read something," he says, "you ask him to take part of the energy of making music and put it somewhere else. Notation can be used as a point of reference, but the notation does not indicate music. It indicates a direction."

In jazz, Taylor has also pointed out, musicians do not waste, as he puts it, their visual energy on matters of notation. They may touch on a score, but by and large, "You look at the instrument and you spend your energy creating sound with the instrument."

Energy. Energy and feeling. Direct feeling. Spontaneously exploding energy. In 1975, in a *Village Voice* interview with Gary Giddins, Taylor elaborated further: "One of the things that turned me off European music is that I'd get the scores by Boulez, Stockhausen, Pousseur, and Ligeti and I would look at them and say, 'My, this is interesting.' And I'd listen to the music and it didn't sound particularly good. I don't listen to artists who only want to create something that is interesting. *To feel is perhaps the most terrifying thing in this society.* This is one of the reasons I'm not too interested in electronic music: it divorces itself from human energy, it substitutes another kind of force as the determinant agent for its continuance."

Force. Energy. Always energy. As a boy, ten or eleven, Cecil had played Mozart. As an adult musician he went to hear Emil Gilels play Mozart at Carnegie Hall. "After the concert," Taylor recalls, "I went down and heard Coltrane who was appearing at the Half Note. And I had to say after about thirty minutes of Coltrane that he had expended more energy, created more music, in maybe two minutes than Gilels spent in an hour and a half."

With John Coltrane dead, Cecil Taylor is the most commanding energy-force in jazz. Eventually other players will emerge with comparable impact, but Cecil Taylor, no more than Coltrane, can never be eclipsed. A product of black traditions, with an admixture of other traditions as well, Taylor has gone on to create and re-create himself, in the process continually mining and expanding his own fiery terrain.

Always, at the unit core of his music, is the naked human spirit and animality. Subtle, incredibly subtle in its nakedness, but naked. How hard Cecil Taylor has striven for the human cry of jazz was indicated, in part, by Buell Neidlinger when he told A. B. Spellman that, when he shared an apartment with Taylor, he saw how Taylor's practicing revolved around solfège singing. "He'll sing a phrase and then he'll harmonize it at the piano and then he'll sing it again, always striving to get the piano to sing, to try and match this feeling of the human production, the voice, in terms of pianistic production so that it gets the same effect. Cecil is trying to get the vocal sound out of the piano, and I think he's achieved it on many occasions. You can almost hear the piano scream or cry."

The distinguished British critic Benny Green, after hearing Cecil Taylor's first recordings in the 1950's, questioned whether what Cecil was doing could even be considered music, let alone jazz. Nearly a quarter-century later, after a Cecil Taylor concert in California at which three thousand people gave him standing, screaming ovations several times during the course of the performance, the distinguished Los Angeles critic Leonard Feather, declared that "anyone working with a jackhammer could have achieved the same musical results."

The problem of defining music, of defining jazz, of understanding the hard exhilaration of this man's music is not Cecil Taylor's problem. "You got to really open up," a musician once told me, "to get into what Cecil's doing. And not everybody wants to open up, I understand that. That can be dangerous. That's why jazz can be dangerous."

jazz is:

International. Everybody knows that.
Compellingly international. During the Second
World War a member of the French underground,
who had been a jazz critic and discographer, was
captured. He was brought to the Gestapo, but
before the heavy questioning began a German
officer, also a jazz discographer, got into an
abstruse, intense conversation with the captive
about the debatable personnel on a rare Bessie
Smith recording.

An American musician just back from a State
Department-sponsored tour of Eastern Europe.
"The guy was from Bulgaria," he said. "I never
got his name. He sat in at a session and man, I've
never heard a piano like that. It was jazz; I mean,

he'd heard it all, from Jelly Roll to Monk, but there was also some wild Bartok-like things and gypsy sounds and rhythms and his own folk music. Somehow it all came together. Not like a pastiche, you know, but really together, really his own. It was scary. Most of those guys, you know, they try to sound like us, and some are very good at it. But this cat is an original. How many more of them are there around the world?"

John Lewis, telling me in 1960: "The originals in jazz, the strong new creators, are no longer going to be of exclusively American origin. There's no telling now where the shaping forces will come from."

the third world cat in the black hat

Gato Barbieri

Sonny Rollins

One sign of John Lewis's prophecy is Gato Barbieri, the most original non-American jazz force since Django Reinhardt and a musician of much greater significance than Reinhardt, for he may herald a new era of the internationalization of jazz. Reinhardt stood alone, but Barbieri is in the vanguard of unpredictable numbers of musicians from various parts of the world who, increasingly, are likely to fuse their own musical heritages with that of jazz and thereby create a multiplicity of new musical languages which would not have existed except for jazz, but which are nourished by a thrusting diversity of other cultural roots as well.

Leandro "Gato" (The Cat) Barbieri. "His physical and spiritual *strength* is staggering," a writer for *Down Beat* proclaimed. "The absolute passion in his sound awakens all the senses."

The Third World Cat in the Black Hat. Always, when he plays, Barbieri wears a wide-brimmed, high-crowned black hat. And he is, quite consciously, of the Third World in his thinking and in his music.

Gato Barbieri was born in Rosario, Argentina, in 1935—a provincial capital better known as the birthplace of Che Guevara. From Rosario to Buenos Aires then to Europe and the United States, Barbieri has engaged in a personal and musical quest of self-discovery that has brought, through his work, a new dimension to the international jazz experience.

This journey has also led him to characterize his music—though it was first shaped by Parker, Davis, and Coltrane—as "Third World." Barbieri notes that "so far as I can recall, the term itself was first used by DeGaulle to represent an independent political force, a third force, between the American and Russian blocs. But after DeGaulle, 'third world' has come to mean the common interests of Asia, Africa, and Latin America. As an Argentinian I am part of the 'Third

World.'"

To understand how this identification has been transmuted by Barbieri into his music, it is necessary to explore the first album of his to have been widely distributed in America, *The Third World*, on Flying Dutchman, and then to go back in order to follow the convoluted route by which this intense musician achieved so provocative a breakthrough for non-American jazz musicians.

At the beginning, jazz was all of music for the young Argentinian. But by the time Barbieri, then in his thirties, had recorded *The Third World*, he had redefined himself and his origins through his music. Though the music remains jazz-powered, there is included, for instance, Villa-Lobos's *Bachianas Brasileiras* which, in a change of rhythm, turns into an African song by Dollar Brand based on a poem by a black South African. There is also a tango by the Argentinian, Astor Piazzola. And before the tango, Barbieri plays flute in an introduction that is the kind of song shepherds in northern Argentina play as they watch their flocks. Furthermore, underneath the bass solo following his flute, one can hear a chantlike song also characteristic of those shepherds. In addition, Barbieri improvises on a typical Brazilian tune, *Zelao*, the story of a man in Rio de Janeiro who has lost his guitar, the only thing he has with which to express himself.

And central to an understanding of Barbieri is the music in that internationally pivotal *Third World* album he has written in homage to Glauber Rocha, a Brazilian filmmaker whose work, vision, and friendship have been a decisive influence on Barbieri. The title of the jazz-inflected music for Rocha, *Antonio das Mortes*, is also the title of a Rocha film which greatly impressed Barbieri.

"The character, Antonio das Mortes," Barbieri told

me, "first appears in an earlier Rocha film, *Black God, White Devil.* In the *sertao*—a grim, desperately poor region in northwest Brazil—Antonio is hired by the state to kill the *cangaceiros* [guerrilla outlaws]. He is highly successful as a killer; but in the subsequent Rocha film, *Antonio das Mortes,* this agent of the state has come to realize that the *cangaceiros* had been fighting on the right side, that they had been fighting for the poor. And so, by the end of the film, Antonio das Mortes has taken a position. He too has become a rebel."

In the music of Antonio das Mortes, Gato Barbieri, on this *Third World* album, is heard saying in the language of Brazil what the leader of the *cangaceiros* screams as he is fatally shot by Antonio at the climax of the earlier film: "Stronger is the power of the people!"

(Frieda Grafe, in *Evergreen Review,* has described Antonio das Mortes: ". . . a giant of a man in a dark-green cape, a purple scarf around his neck, his face—above all, his eyes—concealed by an enormous felt hat under which hangs his long, glistening black hair. He is sinister, he is somber, he is mute." By the end, however, Antonio das Mortes has begun to see his world and himself in a quite different way.)

But how did Gato Barbieri come to comprehend, through jazz, the cultural as well as the political significance of Antonio das Mortes, the shepherd's songs and tangos, and the subtly different rhythms of the Indians of Bolivia, Peru, and Chile which figure increasingly in his later albums?

First, at the age of twelve, he heard Charlie Parker's recording of *Now Is the Time.* Gato had already been playing music—on a small clarinet, a *requinto,* because his hands were small. With jazz becoming an obsession, he moved on to regular clarinet, studying with a private teacher in Buenos Aires, where his family had moved. After five years of clarinet there were three years of alto saxophone lessons and two years of composition study with the composer Juan Carlos Paz.

All this time he was absorbing all he could of jazz. Few records arrived from the source, the United States, but each was eagerly shared and studied by a group of musician friends who felt as strongly as Gato about the music. His wife, Michelle, recalls that Gato was the only jazz musician in Buenos Aires at the time who appreciated Miles Davis. "The others said that Miles didn't swing enough," Michelle adds, "but Gato said that it wasn't only swing that made jazz, that feeling was important, too. Then he fell in love with Coltrane and the same thing happened."

Gato had not actually started playing jazz until he was eighteen, but his proficiency was attained with extraordinary speed and soon he was part of both an orchestra and a small combo led by Lalo Schifrin, who later became a sideman with Dizzy Gillespie and then a remarkably productive Hollywood composer-arranger.

When he was twenty Gato was given a tenor saxophone during a session, and from that point on, drawn by the bigger sound which he felt he needed to express his burgeoning emotions, he concentrated on that instrument.

During these formative years Gato rejected the music of his country. "I didn't listen to or understand the music of Argentina. Jazz was all I thought about, all I valued." Soon the preeminent jazz musician in Argentina, Gato headed his own groups, played on nearly every available jazz recording date and television session, working as well with visiting American jazz performers.

Something essential, however, was lacking—stimulation. His wife, Michelle, born in Buenos Aires, raised in Italy, remembers the dead-end feeling: "There was no competition. No sufficiently challenging new musicians were coming up. We knew Gato had to leave. We spent some seven months in Brazil, but that didn't work out either. It was jazz he was looking for, and so in 1962 we left for Europe."

At first they were based in Rome, where Gato's reputation began to grow as he played in clubs and at the Lugano, San Remo, Bologna, and Milano festivals. He also worked with trumpeter Ted Curson, a Charles Mingus alumnus, and became almost as involved with filmmakers as with musicians. In addition to Rocha, Barbieri has been influenced by filmmakers Gianni Amico and Bernardo Bertolucci. (Gato had already created a sound track in Argentina, and in Italy he was involved in the music for *Before the Revolution*, *L'Harem*, and *La Bella Grinta*, in addition to Gianni Amico's *Notes for a Film on Jazz*. Years later, when Bertolucci wanted "something sublime, very heartbreaking, very lyrical" for the music to *Last Tango in Paris*, he thought of Barbieri, who became responsible for that score, too).

In Rome in the early 1960's Gato's musical influences had spread from Parker, Gillespie, Sonny Rollins, and Coltrane to Ornette Coleman. A key event in Barbieri's development was meeting Don Cherry. "Because Don had been so integral a part of the first recordings by Ornette Coleman," Gato notes, "I wanted very much to play with him. What happened was extraordinary. We met and he invited me to a rehearsal the very next day. And for two years we worked quite steadily throughout Europe. Don also brought me to New York for the first time in 1965, where we recorded *Complete Communion*."

But during these years in Europe, years in which he kept expanding and testing his freedom as a jazz improviser, Gato began to recognize that he had been ignoring his own roots, his own culture. He started to listen, for example, to the tango, realizing that "the way in which authentic tango players tell their stories has the same power, feeling, and spontaneity for them as jazz does for its players."

Later, Glauber Rocha encouraged Barbieri's awakening recognition of the power of his own cultural roots. As Gato's wife, Michelle, told Bob Palmer, a writer for the *New York Times* and *Rolling Stone*, "Gato had never really listened to tango when he was in Argentina because tango was a music for older people and Gato thought only of jazz. Glauber Rocha helped him to understand his relationship to the memories he had of his background, opened him up so that he's not afraid any more of being Argentinian, helped him find an identity he never had before; so much so that when Gato was playing his music in Argentina in 1971—after he had become 'Third World' in his music—the musicians who were really enthusiastic about what he was doing were the old folk musicians, the ones whom Gato at one time didn't pay any attention to. And in recent years Gato has been using more and more of the folk cultures he grew up with."

When I first met Gato in New York, he was well into his Third World music, planning trips back to South America to learn more about—and incorporate into his music—the folk instruments, rhythms, tonal colorations, and expressive forms of other Latin American countries. "The possibilities," he said, "are almost limitless. For one illustration, the Argentine carnivalito rhythm is counted as 2/4 and the Brazilian samba is 2/4 also. But they are completely different. Each South American rhythm has its own particular accentuation.

"It was through jazz," Gato continued, "that I first learned to express myself, but now I know I can be even stronger in that expression if I keep adding to jazz, infusing through jazz all that I can also learn about my own background, my cultural background, in the Third World. I have gone a long way around to discover something that has always been with me but which I thought could only be found somewhere else. Now, so many things are coming together—the blackness of jazz, my own nativeness. It has taken me a long time to get to this stage, but along the way I learned a great deal about myself. And I learned how much there is yet to know. That I will try to discover and say in the music to come."

"It used to be," Michelle Barbieri says, "that Gato wanted very much to be a black jazz musician. But once he understood that *he* had strong cultural roots too and that he came from a part of the world where there is great oppression—as blacks are being oppressed and exploited, and by much the same kind of people—then Gato was able to come into his own."

But what of Gato's Third World music and Gato's Third World politics? He and Michelle are much concerned with the need for fundamental social and political change in the Third World. But he remains essentially an artist. "And that leads," Gato points out, "to a duality that many of us suffer from. An artist can never be a revolutionary. If an artist tries to be a revolutionary he will abuse his art. Can an artist at least *help* make a revolution? No, you can bring revolution into your art, but you can't make a revolution with art. The revolution has to come by political means. But perhaps the music, if it is beautiful enough, can help people begin to change a little bit—begin to change in their consciousness so that they will be ready to move in other ways, political ways. Perhaps. That is all I can say."

A similar question can be asked of the films of an artist such as one of Barbieri's influences, Glauber Rocha, who also has strong political concerns. And a tentative answer has been given by Amos Vogel, the most perceptive of all film critic-historians on the multilayered political implications of movies. Vogel has written of Rocha's films that "especially in

Antonio das Mortes, they assume the flamboyant sweep of revolutionary folk epics, replete with a mysticism both surprising and appropriate for a leftist in the second half of the twentieth century, when rationalism has revealed its limitations, and deeper layers of consciousness and reality are being probed by the new revolutionaries of our day."

And it is in this respect that the music of Gato Barbieri also probes deeper layers of consciousness, beginning with his own. "Where I want to arrive at musically," Gato says, "is the point at which I will be able to express what is in me through the horn as naturally as the act of walking, of breathing. The way it is now, you have a thought and then you proceed to execute it. My dream is to eliminate that step in the process so that the music will flow instantaneously, the music will be so natural that other people will respond to it as naturally as the way it is made. It would be a beginning toward being natural in all things."

At base, *that* kind of liberation is a revolutionary goal which does not, however, require the artist to abuse his art. Quite the opposite. Insofar as powerfully emotional music can help free the self, many selves, from the frozen evasions and sense of impotency and the auto-anesthesia that allow poverty and oppression to go on and on and on, the artist *is* part of a potential revolution. It may all be illusory, but variations of this goal have greatly attracted a number of jazz musicians in different ways, John Coltrane among them. Or, as Gato says, "the music of Coltrane was never explicitly or implicitly political, but it was so profoundly of the spirit, it so deeply expressed the soul of black people, that it could perhaps change people's lives. And that's where certain kinds of revolutions begin."

Like Coltrane's, Barbieri's music, whether "revolutionary" or not in any extramusical sense, is often torrentially lyrical, as in shooting the rapids. But there is a difference. "Like the folk music of African and Latin American drum orchestras," Robert Palmer has pointed out, "it sounds wild and completely improvised but is actually rigorously structured and laid out in advance."

It is music, moreover, specifically influenced by certain ways of filmmaking. "Gato's music is like an arrangement," says Michelle Barbieri, "but instead of writing it all out he structures it in his mind. He *sees* it in sequences, and it has to be exactly like that. The segments are flexible and the musicians can open them up, but there is always a definite structure, a story to be told. So the music has the rigorousness of Latin-American folk music, the storytelling narrative structure which comes from films, and the improvisation which comes from jazz."

To which Gato adds: "And there are parts of the music which need words to be better understood. So I sing sometimes, not because I like to but because the music needs singing. And when I scream with my horn, it's because the music needs screaming."

As more Third World jazz emerges in the decades ahead, much of it is likely to consist of music that needs screaming. It will be instructive to see how much of it governments in various Third World countries will allow to be performed at home. There are those who do think that jazz, including Third World jazz, can be dangerous.

"Meanwhile," says Michelle Barbieri, "Gato wants to put together a new group that will express the complete sound of the Latin American Third World. We're going to go from country to country until we find the right people."

There are, after all, all kinds of revolutions.

jazz is:

Duke Ellington telling what went into his *Harlem Air Shaft:* "So much goes on in a Harlem air shaft, You get the full sense of Harlem in an air shaft. You hear fights, you smell dinner, you hear people making love. You hear intimate gossip floating down. You hear the radio. An air shaft is one big loudspeaker. You see your neighbor's laundry. You hear the janitor's dogs. The man upstairs' aerial falls down and breaks your window. You smell coffee. A wonderful thing, that smell. An air shaft has got every contrast. One guy is cooking dried fish and rice and another guy's got a great big turkey. Guy-with-fish's wife is a terrific cooker but the guy's wife with the turkey is doing a sad job. You hear people praying, fighting, snoring. Jitterbugs are jumping up and down always over you, never below you. . . . I tried to put all that in *Harlem Air Shaft*."

Archie Shepp: "You whites own the music and we make it. By definition, then, you own the people who make the music. You own us in whole chunks of flesh."

Jimmy Owens, trumpeter, speaking for *Collective Black Artists* (an organization of black musicians begun in New York): "Black music has never really been controlled by the people who are making that music. Consequently, the amount of money going to the people who perform that music, the musicians, has been very small compared to what goes to the people who control the music."

the political economy of jazz

Dizzy Gillespie and Max Roach

Donald Byrd

One of the innumerable, immemorial myths about jazz is that before bop (the modern era) began, black players and performers did not think politically about the music. It was a living, a craft, and, to be sure, a most distinctive way of expression with its own aesthetic criteria. (It don't mean a thing, Mr. Paul Whiteman, if you ain't got that swing, and you don't.) But as for black consciousness in the contemporary sense—"This is *our* music and we ought to control it"—well, the white legend goes, black jazzmen weren't that hip that soon. They just cared about blowing, you know, and making some kind of bread.

In truth, Duke Ellington, as noted above, came to Fletcher Henderson in the late 1920's with a proposition. Much was being made at the time of Paul Whiteman bringing "dignity" to jazz, and Ellington said to Henderson, "Look, why don't we drop the word 'jazz'? Let's call what we're doing 'Negro music' and then there won't be any confusion between what we do and what Whiteman and all the other white men do." Henderson, a cautious man, declined that venturesome a place in history. And Duke went on writing and playing his black music, seldom if ever using the term "jazz."

Duke was hardly alone. In the thirty-five years or so that I've hung out, from time to time, with jazz musicians, I was often instructed in the political economy of jazz long before I knew such current bringers of the angry word as Max Roach, Miles Davis, Cecil Taylor, and Archie Shepp. When I was a teenager, Frankie Newton and Rex Stewart, among others, gave me noncredit courses in the dynamics of the real jazz life by contrast with the one I idealized.

"Where the control is, the money is," Rex began, primer-style. "Do you see any of us running any record companies, booking agencies, radio stations, music magazines?"

And later, "Do you see any of us with any power in the schools and the colleges? So long as kids don't know what this music is all about, where it comes from, it's going to keep on being merchandised as 'entertainment' on the same level as hoofers and acrobats. And when I say kids, I mean black kids, too. Ellington is the goddamn Beethoven of this country. You think they teach Ellington's music in the schools?"

Of course, there were black kids and older blacks who knew the nonpareil value of Ellington, even if they didn't find that out in a school. And some whites knew. But it was surely true that black musicians were under white control. And it was also true that jazz lacked official legitimacy. Growing up, I was an addicted reader of such of the "high culture" journals as *Kenyon Review, Partisan Review, Sewanee Review,* et al.; and to those empyrean tastemakers, jazz, or any kind of black music, hardly existed at all. Maybe one piece every five years in one of those magazines. And then, of course, by a white prehipster, a white Negro.

The ignorance of black music among members of the white cultural establishment was—and still largely is—stunningly dismaying. Talk about two separate nations. Or, as the late Ralph Gleason pointed out in his book, *Celebrating The Duke and Louis, Bessie, Billie, Bird, Carmen, Miles, Dizzy, and Other Heroes:* "When Lyndon Johnson gave his celebrated culture cocktail party, Dwight Macdonald . . . wrote a long piece in the *New York Review of Books* lamenting that among all the artists gathered in Washington that fateful day there were no American composers. Then, as I read on, Macdonald described how the best moment of the entire affair was when Duke Ellington's magnificent orchestra played for the guests. It was a profound shock to realize that Duke Ellington . . . was not even *considered* a composer by Dwight Macdonald."

Of course, he wasn't considered a composer by Macdonald. Duke was considered a lively black entertainer. Why should an expert in American culture know of *Black Beauty; Black, Brown and Beige; Deep South Suite; Harlem Air Shaft?* And if Dwight Macdonald didn't know, who in the schools would know?

At one point I decided to become some kind of expert on the nation's indigenous culture and won a fellowship to Harvard Graduate School, where I embarked on a Ph.D. program in American civilization. My notion that black music might be part of this course of studies was considered at best impudent frivolity on my part. I was allowed, however, to do a paper on Phyllis Wheatley, the eighteenth-century Boston slave-poet. One night I dropped out of graduate school, having decided that hearing Sidney Bechet at the Savoy Cafe in Boston that very evening was much more central to my understanding of American civilization than the paper on James Fenimore Cooper I had been mandated to write. Actually it had come to me that my priorities were not those of a putative professor. At least not by the standards of the academy at the time; and those standards have not changed significantly.

Anyway, along came modern jazz and there was indeed a change in the consciousness of black jazz musicians even though that of white cultural arbiters remained frozen. Many older players had been acutely conscious of the cultural value of what they were doing—and of the exploitation by whites of what they were doing—but they had often acted as entertainers because that's how they got paid. Now there was to be a different, sometimes abrasive, stance. As pianist-composer John Lewis observed: "This revolution, or whatever you want to call it, in the 1940's took place for many reasons, and not only for musical reasons. . . . For the younger musicians, this was the way to react against the attitude that Negroes were supposed to entertain people. The new attitude of these young Negroes was: 'Either you listen to me on the basis of what I actually do or forget it.' "

And that's how Charlie Parker played, and Miles Davis, and a lot more. And with this attitude came a most specific articulation of economic grievances. As Max Roach put it: "We invented, we created the music. . . . Hell, man, this is black classical music. White classical musicians get many more times the advance money that we get. But black music has to be wholly self-supporting. So much of that European classical stuff, on the other hand, is on relief, subsidized by foundations, state commissions and things."

The new breed—new in their activism—have since worked to change the political economy of jazz. Some independent record labels owned by black musicians have been started, and while they do provide essential outlets for diversely adventurous music which established labels would not be likely to record, these black firms remain constricted because the white-run record distribution system has less than minimal interest in so "special" a product. Accordingly, the black labels make whatever deals they can, set up their own small distribution networks, or sell by mail. Meanwhile, although there are some blacks working for the established record companies now, they are far from positions of control.

Then there is the question of the schools. Here and there around the country, black musicians have entered local school systems and, with some success, are involving kids from first grade on with the actual making of jazz. But they are still few.

More characteristic of the state of black music in the

schools is what's happening at an impressive black elementary school in Dayton. The black principal has high expectations of the kids and insists that these expectations be shared by her staff. She also considers it important for the kids to know their heritage, as she puts it; and so posters abound of black doctors and scientists and Martin Luther King and, yes, Malcolm X too. But I saw no black musicians on the school walls—no Duke or Basie or Bessie Smith or Billie Holiday or Dizzy Gillespie or John Coltrane. When I asked about the absence of jazz personages, the principal looked at me as if I were quite daft. "Why, those are show people. We want people who have accomplished things."

A couple of days after Charlie Parker died, Art Blakey, a drummer who specializes in accomplishing things, said sadly and angrily: "Most black kids in school today don't even know who Charlie Parker was." Same with most white kids in school. Blakey's comment brought me back to American Civilization at Harvard.

As did a report from Marian McPartland. She likes to proselytize for jazz in schools, and a few years ago was working in a nearly all-black school in Washington, D.C. A persistent woman, Marian prevailed on Duke Ellington to visit one afternoon, talk with the kids, play for them. Preliminarily, she asked the students what compositions of his, what Ellington recordings, they especially liked. Most of them had never heard any music by Duke, and many knew him, if at all, in the same blurred way they might know the name of a vaguely historic prime minister of England.

Angry at the void, there have been black musicians who decided to move onto college faculties where they could teach music to prospective musicians and scholars—and to teachers in the lower schools. One of them, trumpeter Donald

Byrd, headed a jazz department at Howard University for a time. This was the same university which, for decades (like other black institutions of higher learning) had forbidden the teaching of jazz, the blues, and other ways of black music which did not meet white standards of "high culture." It was at Howard that, decades ago, English professor and poet Sterling Brown, black and an expert on the blues, had to sneak jazz into the curriculum by playing recordings of jazz-influenced works by Stravinsky and Milhaud, and then enabling the students to hear where they'd come from by putting on "supplementary" recordings of the real thing.

Byrd set up a curriculum at Howard, and himself having been well initiated into how jazz musicians are exploited, he insisted on including a course, "Legal Protection of the Arts," which involved, among other things, the art of self-defense in negotiating contracts. Meanwhile, Byrd was also touring other black campuses, advising administrators on how to set up their own black music divisions.

On one such trip, as he told me, Byrd ran into a rather classic instance of how durable cultural colonialism can be. Arriving at the campus, he was greeted by a black senior professor of music who was lamenting the fact that, as he put it, "I can't get my students to listen to *good* music."

"What exactly do you mean?" Byrd asked.

"You understand," the professor said. "Bach, Beethoven, Brahms."

Byrd stared coldly at the faculty member. "I wasn't quite sure what I was going to lecture about tonight," he said, "but now I know. *You* are going to be the subject of my lecture. Your narrow, uptight, European standards of what's 'good' in music. Wake up, man. Wake up to black music."

More black jazz musicians than anyone in the late

'30's would have thought possible are now in the academy. There are and have been black music courses and sometimes departments at, among other places, Bowdoin, Brandeis, Antioch, the University of Wisconsin, Dartmouth, Wesleyan, the State University of New York at Old Westbury, Indiana University, the University of Pittsburgh, Brown, and the University of Massachusetts at Amherst.

A good many of the black musicians involved in such ventures feel, with sound reason, that they are isolated from the rest of the university. They are also not sanguine about their chances of getting a tenure line, because how "serious" a contribution to the university can black music be regarded on high? And almost without exception they are aware of the disdain with which they and their music are regarded by most of the white members of the established music departments.

Clearly, it is going to be a continual struggle to safeguard, let alone expand, college and university centers of black music. And the main reason, again, is that most whites who have anything to do with education are nearly totally ignorant of the significance and the very nature of black music.

Composer-teacher David Baker, who has had more experience trying to implant black music in the academy than almost anyone else, has noted in *Black World* that: "If a student of jazz (teacher, performer, neophyte, etc.) were to exhibit the same kind of total ignorance about Western art music that most members of the musical establishment exhibit toward jazz, he would be termed a musical illiterate. Yet there are Ph.D. candidates who pride themselves on their ability to recall facts about the most remote and obscure 15th-century composer, 17th-century theoretical treatise or lost opera, but know nothing of the musical importance of John Coltrane, Charlie Parker, Dizzy Gillespie or George Russell. (All of these men have contributed greatly to the advancement of world music.)"

The measure should extend farther, however. Not only doctoral candidates in music ought to know (if only in self-respect) the work of Coltrane, Parker, Gillespie, et al. Anyone involved in American history, sociology, and the study of political economy, is professionally and culturally deprived if he or she is without substantive knowledge of jazz, of black music. But how many faculty members—in secondary schools and up—could pass even a simple quiz on the cultural history of jazz?

Meanwhile, however, there appears to be a resurgence of interest in jazz among the young. Nothing phenomenal, but encouraging. One index of that rise in interest is that students, if not faculty, are attending jazz classes—where they exist—like those taught by Professor Ted Wilson, Jr.

A few years ago, encouraged by what at the time appeared to be a civil-rights and black-culture "revolution," a young black pianist-composer asked, 'If a place like Lincoln Center can be built for classical music, why can't another place be built for a music that is a product of this society?" The question has yet to be answered.

Things Ain't What They Used to Be says a Duke Ellington song. But in this respect they ain't that much different for jazz. Oh, the music keeps changing, but not, so you'd notice it, the political economy of the music. And in the schools black and white kids alike still get to appreciate the hell out of the music of dead Europeans.

jazz is:

Dizzy Gillespie, smiling, telling a twenty-year-old trumpet player: "It's taken me all my life to learn what not to play."

John Lewis, teaching "A History of Jazz from World War II to the Present"—the first course at Harvard University to be devoted to jazz—is asked by a student about the origins of Dizzy Gillespie's *A Night in Tunisia*. Why, in sum, did Dizzy write it?

"Well, he was glad to write it for a record date," Lewis, smiling, answers. "The best inspiration is to write for pay."

Don Cherry: "I dig to play Monk because Monk's tunes make you improvise on melody and not on chords. They have you thinking without thinking, like some kind of conscious unconscious. Or something."

Sonny Rollins, conducting a master class for three students at Howard University: "Sometimes I'm able to step outside myself and hear what I'm playing. The ideas just flow. The horn and I become one."

Bessie Smith, as John Hammond tells her he has engaged Big Sid Catlett for her record date: "I don't want no drummer. *I* set the tempo."

Big Sid Catlett: "I can swing seventeen men with one wire brush and a phone book."

Cecil Taylor, telling British interviewer Les Tomkins that in his formative years "I began listening to Cab Calloway, Chick Webb, Fats Waller, Duke Ellington, and Jimmie Lunceford. Yes, I would say they inspired me."

"At the time," Tomkins asks, "was it the kind of inspiration that made you want to play the same way as them?"

"Well," says Cecil Taylor, "they were beacons, lights indicating a certain direction. There was a certain kind of cloth that they wore, that was manifested in the sounds that came out of their being. There was a way that they looked, a way that you felt when you heard what they did, that you wanted to become a part of. And you strove to *become* a part of it. It's a question of trying to achieve that image in sound, in thought, in feeling, in being."

Anthony Braxton, like Cecil Taylor an avant-gardist, in *Coda:* "There's a lot of creative music happening in the underground, which is a very hopeful kind of sign. . . . [These initiators are] usually kind of outcasts—for the most part no one can relate to them. And it's all over the planet; you go and look in the alleys and under the doorways, in the coal mines—they're there, lurking in the shadows: a significant amount of people in different parts of the planet who are genuinely creative. And I associate and attach myself to that.

"Usually when I go to any new place I try to find out from the musicians—they'll usually say something like 'this guy can't play,' or 'he's crazy,' 'he's not doing anything,' 'he's a sick, warped, demented fool'—and immediately I try to find him. He's probably one of us."

Barry Altschul, percussionist: "There was a period during which I got into playing the sounds of the street. I started digging the sounds of everyday, street noises—trucks and rain and trains and crashes and sirens and horns. I started listening to the ocean, too. I started to hear these sounds as music, and they began to have a place in *my* music."

last (open-ended) chorus

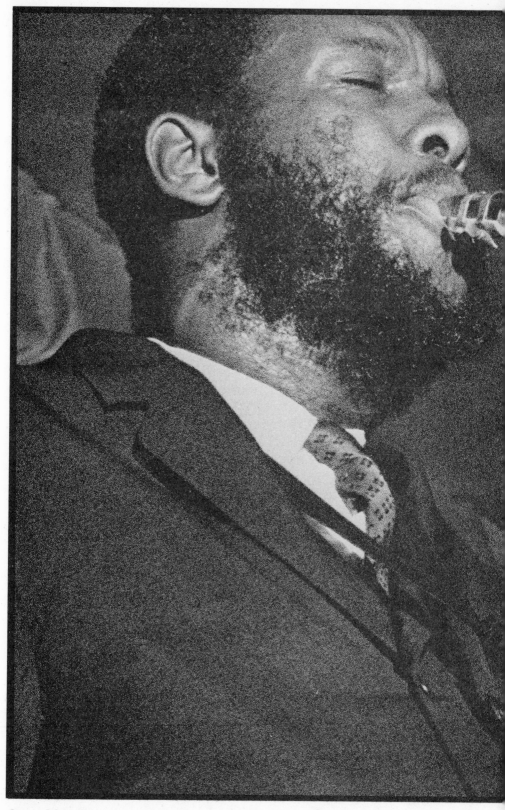

Ornette Coleman

Roy Eldridge

A life work, a music that is the player's life, is shaped by that life and shapes the life in turn. A work. A continual honing. For some a continual expanding, searching. Beyond notes into sounds. Thinking without thinking, the horn and player become one. A hard way up for the strange player who then becomes the norm as stranger players lurk in the shadows. A music that is celebration, and part of what it celebrates is its history, its rich, dense, quite thrilling history of players whose way of walking as well as sounding were beacons, lights indicating a certain direction.

Young players now, perhaps more than ever before, are digging into the history of the music while simultaneously reaching and sounding farther ahead. Leo Smith, a trumpet player who for some years was a key element in the Chicago-based Association for the Advancement of Creative Music, has read widely and listened deeply in the tradition, and he speaks knowledgeably of Johnny and Baby Dodds and Louis Armstrong and the all-black World War I Army band of James Reese Europe.

In an interview in the Canadian jazz journal, *Coda*, Smith proudly reports that when James Reese Europe's band toured the Continent, it found skeptics among French musicians who could only explain the vital difference in the music of these black players by the theory that their instruments had been adapted to sound as they did. And so, Smith says, the French players switched instruments with the black musicians, but the French players still sounded as they had, and the improvising blacks still sounded as *they* had. Well, then, the French musicians said, it must be the music scores. So they switched their music with that of the black players, but the blacks made the French scores sound black and the French players could not make the black players' music sound hot.

And they certainly could not make it swing.

Smith's story reminded me of Pee Wee Russell's attempt, years ago, to define jazz: "You could use ten-syllable words and it wouldn't mean a thing. If I say something in the way of a definition I'd probably retract it a second later. I'm not sure this will do it, but in a way it comes down to this—a certain group of guys—I don't care where they come from—that have a heart feeling and a rhythm in their systems that you couldn't budge, a rhythm you couldn't take away from them even if they were in a symphony organization. Regardless of what type of music they decided to play, they could feel a beat from the conductor. They could feel the beat better than someone who has memorized the book. These are men whose way of playing you couldn't alter no matter where you put them or what you tried to teach them."

That's part of it. And so is the continuous creation and re-creation of "legitimacy" in sound, in structure, in the very definition of all elements of music. The earliest players, "the singing horns," initiated, out of the urgency of expression, colorations and ways of phrasing and of bending notes, extensions of range, and myriad other permutations of sound that had never been heard before. And it's been that way ever since.

Trombonist Grachan Moncur III has emphasized, "If it's necessary to use an extended technique to express what I'm trying to say, I'll do it. If I have to bang on a dishpan with a stick, I'll do that, too." Or, as reedman James Moody observes, "*Any* sound makes sense to me. Any sound at all. You fell on the floor—it makes sense. You *fell*, didn't you? Music is supposed to represent a feeling."

So it is that the post-bop players, though so much more sophisticated musically than their prejazz ancestors, are still linked to those Southern black post-Civil War musicians who had no lesson books and accordingly turned horns into extensions of the human voice—slurring, burring, braying, crying. The late Eric Dolphy, one of the most daring of all the younger jazz experimenters, was once startled and pleased when he experienced a sudden recognition of this bond between him and the past. As a participant in a Washington, D.C., jazz festival, Dolphy heard the Eureka Jazz Band of New Orleans for the first time. "I stood right in the middle of those old men," Dolphy recalled, "and I couldn't see much difference from what I'm doing, except that they were blowing tonally, but with lots of freedom. You know something? They were the first freedom players."

And since there never is enough freedom, jazz has been a history of generations of freedom players. Ornette Coleman, for one. Coming up, Ornette—like Cecil Taylor, like others who have heard possibilities beyond the imaginings of the established players—was scorned for a long time. One leader paid him *not* to play; at jam sessions, musicians nearly stalked off the stand when Ornette walked on. But he stubbornly kept developing music he felt had to come into being. "Music," Ornette said in the early 1960's, "is for our feelings. I think jazz should try to express more kinds of feelings than it has up to now. For instance, there are some intervals that carry the *human* quality if you play them in the right pitch. You can reach into the sound of a human voice on your horn if you're actually hearing and trying to express the warmth of a human voice."

In addition to his breakthroughs in textures, Coleman—along with (in their ways) Miles Davis, John Coltrane, and others—also helped lead the way to the jettisoning of traditional chordal supports for improvisers. Without having to continually touch base within a preset harmonic framework, his melodies soared and careened with unprecedented freedom, creating different kinds of inner relations, relationships of pitch, emotion, and rhythm.

Coleman's use of rhythm was another influence on what became the new jazz of the 1970's (except that most of its black players call it "black music" or "creative music"). Listening to him is one way to begin to understand and feel the rhythmic liberation that is still going on.

"My music," Ornette Coleman once pointed out, "doesn't have any real time, no metric time. It has time, but not in the sense that you can time it. It's more like breathing—a natural, freer time. People have forgotten how beautiful it is to be natural. I like spread rhythm—rhythm that has a lot of freedom in it—rather than the more conventional netted rhythm. With spread rhythm, you might tap your feet a while, then stop, then later start tapping again. Otherwise, you tap your feet so much, you forget what you hear. You just hear the rhythm."

Rhythmically, the newer jazz has become even more open to possibilities. The beat is seldom explicitly stated. Instead, rhythm sections produce continually shifting, overlapping, complexly intersecting layers. For a listener the feeling may be that of plunging into vortices of colliding pulsations, and it may require almost as much concentration to be aware of and responsive to all that's happening as it would to be a participating player. And bassist Eddie Gomez, best known internationally for his work with Bill Evans, predicts: "We're only on the surface level of what *can* be done. Break that surface, and there's a whole lot more underneath. There's no basic rhythm to do it for you—you have to be a world within yourself."

Altogether, the gestalt of the new jazz can either be enormously energizing for the listener, or dismayingly confusing, depending on how open he is to the unexpected and how willing he is to keep listening until coherence does emerge. Sometimes it won't, because some "free form" players are hustlers—poor or lazy musicians who hope that their squawking and yowling will get by as a part of the new freedom. But, as Jo Jones said decades ago, there's no place to hide in jazz. If some listeners are fooled, the authentic innovators will not be; and as always in jazz history those players will last who are sooner or later chosen by unmistakably real originators to work with them. So John Coltrane put an imprimatur on younger musicians. So now do graduates of the Association for the Advancement of Creative Music (and other postgraduate players like Marion Brown) show who's worth paying attention to by whom they select to play with. Always pay heed to the musicians rather than the critics.

And some musicians will have to prove themselves all alone, as Cecil Taylor has. But even in his case there were a few musicians all along the way who knew the nonpareil value of his work.

Often now the new jazz moves forward in dense thickets of sound. Sometimes it is impossible to listen for melodic lines, in the usual sense, in the ensemble passages. But the torrents of sound, boiling with emotion, achieve cohesion if one listens in a different way.

"Don't always focus on the notes, on what sequence they'd be in if you were to write them down," advises Don Ayler, the trumpet-playing brother of the late Albert Ayler, a searingly influential saxophonist. "Instead try to move your imagination toward the sound. Follow the sound, the pitches, the colors. You have to almost watch them move. You have to try to listen to everything together."

And so, of course, does the musician have to listen to everything together. A few years ago, vibist Bobby Hutcherson described the degree of concentration required of the players in the new music. "For me," he said, "there's no challenge like being part of what's happening in jazz now. You really find out how creative you are, how much music you know. Like you're out there, and you know there's no chord pattern where you can say, 'Okay, on this D-minor 7th chord I'm going to play . . . ,' or 'Yeah, I know this lick, I can run across that, and then I can do that.' It's not like that. You're out there, and you have to listen. You have to have your ears as wide open as you possibly can, listening to everything else as much as possible, and at the same time concentrating on what you're trying to do. It makes you so much more involved in what's going on. If you even think about anything but the music, you're going to miss the whole thing. You're going to miss so much."

Just as involved, still, are many of the older jazz players. Those of whom Cecil Taylor has said: "They laid down the lore as well as the law, you know, and the aesthetic standards that were achieved in their playing under all kinds of conditions are what we carry with us. They have become part of our commitment."

As at Preservation Hall in New Orleans where, in the spring of 1975, I heard Jim Robinson, then eighty-four, playing a glowing, burry trombone solo, the horn an extension of him, the horn moving as his body moved. And Robinson smiling as the audience smiled and applauded. The music young in the old man who had said a while back, "I like to see people happy. If everybody is in a frisky spirit, the spirit gets to me and I can make my trombone sing. If my music makes people happy, I will try to do more. It is a challenge to me. I always want people around me. It gives me a warm heart and that gets into my music. When I play sweet music, I try to give my feelings to the other fellow. That's always in my mind. Everybody in the world should know this."

The whole Preservation Hall Jazz Band was full of the spirit, most of its members in their sixties and seventies but getting through, with ease and confidence, to kids as well as to the kids' parents sitting eagerly in the hall. And when they themselves had been kids, these New Orleans musicians-to-be had been part of an ambience once described by Danny Barker as being like a sonic aurora borealis—"A bunch of us kids, playing, would suddenly hear sounds. The sounds of men playing. They'd be so clear, but we wouldn't be sure where they were coming from. So we'd start trotting, start running—'It's this way! It's that way!' And sometimes, after running for a while, you'd find you'd be nowhere near that music. But that music could come on you any time like that. The city was full of the sounds of music."

No wonder that, as another elderly New Orleans musician has said, "the most miserable feeling a youngster in New Orleans could experience was to be in a classroom in school, studying, and hear a brass band approach, swinging like crazy, pass the school, and fade off in the distance."

Jazz is the Pied Piper's music. Once it has seized you, you'll never have enough of it, as a listener and most certainly as a player. Roy Eldridge, for instance, playing as fiercely, as competitively, as he was decades ago while besting all comers at jam sessions until Dizzy Gillespie dethroned him.

When Roy was fifty, I wrote about a record session I had produced with him and Charles Mingus. At the end of the date Roy said to Mingus, with whom he had never before recorded: "I'm glad I made this. I wanted to find out what bag you're in. Now I know you're in the right bag. There are some people coming up who are so busy being busy on their horns that they forget the basics. They don't get all the way down into the music. You did, baby. It's good to know. There are very few of us left out here."

Roy, at the time, was so out of fashion that when, a couple of weeks after the record session, the 1960 *Down Beat* readers' poll came out, he was nowhere to be found in the trumpet list, even though it took only fifteen votes to get a place on the rolls. He never told me how he felt about that, but Roy continued to refuse to go gently into limbo, blowing and swinging with intensity, and sometimes exaltation.

At that record session with Mingus several young modern jazz players had been hanging around the studio. One of them, a Dizzy Gillespie disciple, kept shaking his head at what and how Eldridge was playing. "He may not be hip," said the modernist of Eldridge, "but Jesus, he sure fills that horn."

A few minutes later, Eldridge unleashed a ferocious, cracklingly hot solo and then, laughing, pointed to the youngster and said, "We're still trying, aren't we?"

And fifteen years later, at the Montreux Jazz Festival with Dizzy Gillespie, Roy was *still* trying. As British journalist Benny Green wrote: ". . . Roy had been playing, Dizzy resting, and there had arrived one moment when Roy, practically coming apart at the seams with aspiring ambition, went for some crystalline epigram of his youth far up in the higher reaches of his instrument, and getting close enough to it for the experienced listener to pick up the allusion—at which point Diz, who had been passing the TV monitor in the band-room, and had been arrested in mid-saunter, as it were, by the spectacle of his old hero continuing to be heroic, turned to all the other musicians watching, and smiled that peculiarly significant smile which professionals are inclined to use when they want to say something like, 'How about that?' "

Roy, "Little Jazz," on fire with jazz, like Jim Robinson in New Orleans dancing with his trombone and shouting to the band, "Let's go!" Like Cecil Taylor, leaping across precipices made of his own imagination every time he plays. They are all jazz.

A reporter from *Izvestia* approaches Norman Granz, who is with Oscar Peterson on a tour of the U.S.S.R., and asks Granz which musician most typifies jazz for him.

Granz recalls: "Oscar was whispering to me, 'Tatum. Tatum. Tell him it's Tatum.' I said, 'No, it's Roy Eldridge who embodies what jazz is all about. He's a musician for whom it's far more important to dare, to try to achieve a particular peak—even if he falls on his ass in the attempt—than it is to play safe. That's what jazz is all about."

Always has been and continues to be. There is, of course, no one embodiment of jazz. But there is, I think, one quintessential definition of jazz—of all eras and styles, past and future. Jimmy McPartland, the vintage trumpeter, remembers: "People used to ask Bix Beiderbecke to play a chorus just as he had recorded it. He couldn't do it. 'It's impossible,' he told me once. 'I don't feel the same way twice. That's one of the things I like about jazz, kid. I don't know what's going to happen next. Do you?'"

discography

A selective guide to jazz recordings
Like this book, this list is not meant to be comprehensive
but is intended as a foundation on which a jazz collection can be built.

To begin with, the best single introduction to the sound
of jazz is *The Smithsonian Collection of Classic Jazz,* assembled and
annotated by Martin Williams, Director of the Jazz Program,
Smithsonian Institution, Washington, D.C. 20560. A boxed collection
of six LPs, encompassing 84 recordings, the collection ranges
from Scott Joplin to Cecil Taylor.

Armstrong, Louis, *Louis Armstrong and Earl Hines,* Smithsonian
    Collection R002 (not included in the above set)
Armstrong, Louis, *Plays W. C. Handy,* Columbia Special Products, JCL-591
Armstrong, Louis, *Louis Armstrong Story,* Columbia CL 851-854
Barbieri, Gato, *Latin America,* Impulse 9248
Barbieri, Gato, *Hasta Siempre,* Impulse 9263
Barbieri, Gato, *Viva Emiliano Zapata,* Impulse 9279
Basie, Count (trio), *"For The First Time,"* Pablo 2310 712
Basie, Count, *The Best of Count Basie,* MCA 4050E
Bechet, Sidney, *Master Musician,* Bluebird AXM2-5516
Coleman, Ornette, *Shape of Jazz to Come,* Atlantic S-1317
Coltrane, John, *Ascension,* Impulse S-95
Coltrane, John, *Giant Steps,* Atlantic S-1311
Coltrane, John, *Live at the Village Vanguard,* Atlantic S-10
Davis, Miles, *Bitches Brew,* Columbia PG-26
Davis, Miles, *Kind of Blue,* Columbia PC-8163
Davis, Miles, *Complete Birth of the Cool,* Capitol M-11026
Davis, Miles, *Sketches of Spain,* Columbia PC-8271
Davis, Miles, *Steamin' with Coltrane,* Prestige S-7580
Eldridge, Roy, *Happy Time,* Pablo 2310-739
Ellington, Duke, *The Ellington Era,* Columbia C3L-27
Ellington, Duke, *Tone Parallel to Harlem/Liberian Suite,* Columbia J-6
Ellington, Duke, *At His Very Best,* RCA LPM-1715
Ellington, Duke (trio), *This One's for Blanton,* Pablo 2310-721

Gillespie, Dizzy, *In the Beginning*, Prestige P-24030

Gillespie, Dizzy, *At the French Riviera*, Philips 600048

Gillespie, Dizzy, *Oscar Peterson & Dizzy Gillespie*, Pablo 2310-740

Holiday, Billie, *Golden Years, Vols. I and II*, Columbia C3L-21, C3L-40

Holiday, Billie, *God Bless the Child*, Columbia PG-30782

Holiday, Billie, *The Billie Holiday Story*, Columbia PG-32121,
    PG-32124, PG-32127

Mingus, Charles, *Blues & Roots*, Atlantic S-1305

Mingus, Charles, *Mingus Ah Um*, Columbia CS-8171

Mingus, Charles, *Tia Juana Moods*, RCA APL 1-0939

Mingus, Charles, *Tonight at Noon*, Atlantic S-1416

Modern Jazz Quartet, *Last Concert*, Atlantic 909

Monk, Thelonious, *Brilliance*, Milestone 47023

Monk, Thelonious, *Monk/Trane*, Milestone M-47011

Mulligan, Gerry, *Mulligan/Konitz-Revelation*, Blue Note BN-LA-532-H2

Mulligan, Gerry, *Quartet/Desmond Quintet*, Fantasy 8082

Mulligan, Gerry, *Jeru*, Columbia Special Products, CSP JCS-8732

Mulligan, Gerry, *Age of Steam*, A&M 3036

Parker, Charlie, *Bird/The Savoy Recordings*, Savoy SJL 2201

Parker, Charlie, *Charlie Parker on Dial*, Vols. 1–6, Spotlite 101–106

Parker, Charlie, *Bird & Diz* [Gillespie], Verve 68006

Parker, Charlie, *Charlie Parker*, Prestige 24009

Smith, Bessie, *The Bessie Smith Story*, Columbia 855-858

Smith, Bessie, *The World's Greatest Blues Singer*, Columbia GP-33

Taylor, Cecil, *In Transition*, Blue Note LA458-H2

Taylor, Cecil, *Looking Ahead*, Contemporary 7562

Taylor, Cecil, *Café Montmartre*, Fantasy 86014

Taylor, Cecil, *Unit Structures*, Blue Note 84237

Taylor, Cecil, *Silent Tongues*, Arista/Freedom 1005

Waller, Fats, *The Complete Fats Waller, Vol. 1*, Bluebird AXM2-5511

Wilson, Teddy, *And His All-Stars*, Columbia 31617

Wilson, Teddy, *Piano Solos*, Columbia J-8

Wilson, Teddy, *Moonglow*, Black Lion 177

Wilson, Teddy, *With Billie in Mind*, Chiaroscuro 111

bibliography

Balliett, Whitney. *Dinosaurs in the Morning.* Philadelphia:
     J. B. Lippincott, 1962.

Balliett, Whitney. *The Sound of Surprise.* New York: E. P. Dutton, 1959.

Bechet, Sidney. *Treat It Gentle.* New York: Hill & Wang, 1960.

Dance, Stanley. The World of Duke Ellington. New York:
     Charles Scribner's, 1970.

Ellison, Ralph. *Shadow and Act.* New York: Random House, Vintage [paperback], 1964.

Gold, Robert S. *Jazz Talk.* New York: Bobbs-Merrill, 1975.

Hentoff, Nat and Shapiro, Nat, editors. *Hear Me Talkin' to Ya.* New
     York: Holt, Rinehart and Winston, Dover [paperback], 1955.

Hentoff, Nat. *The Jazz Life.* New York: Dial Press, 1961. Reprint,
     New York: Da Capo Press, 1975.

Hodeir, André. *Jazz: Its Evolution and Essence.* New York: Grove Press, 1956.

Jones, LeRoi. *Black Music.* New York: William Morrow, 1967.

Jones, LeRoi. *Blues People.* New York: William Morrow, 1963.

Mellers, Wilfred. *Music in a New Found Land.* New York: Hillstone, 1975.

Mingus, Charles. *Beneath the Underdog.* New York: Alfred A. Knopf, 1971.

Reisner, Robert. *Bird: The Legend of Charlie Parker.*
     New York: The Citadel Press, 1962.

Russell, Ross. *Bird Lives!* New York: Charterhouse, 1973.

Schuller, Gunther. *Early Jazz: Its Roots and Musical
     Development.* New York: Oxford University Press, 1968.

Simpkins, Dr. C. D. *Coltrane: A Biography.* New York: Herndon House, 1975.

Spellman, A.B. *Four Lives in the BeBop Business.* New York:
     Pantheon, 1966. Also available in paperback, *Black Music:
     Four Lives.* New York: Schocken, 1970.

Thomas, J.C. *Chasin' The Trane: The Music and Mystique of
     John Coltrane.* New York: Doubleday, 1975.

Williams, Martin. *The Jazz Tradition.* New York: Oxford
     University Press, 1970.

Williams, Martin. *Where's the Melody?* New York: Pantheon,
     Revised edition, 1969.

index